St Irenaeus

Icon of St Irenaeus, Bishop of Lyon, c.180 AD
Written by Helen Daylon, 2017

Making sense of things

through the lens of Christian belief

Paul Burt

Making Sense of Things through the lens of Christian belief

Copyright © 2023 Paul Burt

ISBN: 9798389989047

All rights reserved. No part of this book may be reproduced, scanned or transmitted in any form, digital, audio or printed, without the express written consent of the author.

Contents

Preface	1
1 Time	12
2 Nature	44
3 Language	80
4 Person	120

Preface

One of the most famous atheists in recent British history was the playwright, physician, theatre director, actor and public intellectual Jonathan Miller. Some years ago he was interviewed by a journalist during a stroll around Miller's *alma mater*, Cambridge University. He and the interviewer were walking together in the famous chapel of King's College, marveling at the wonderful architecture and stained glass. Miller talked enthusiastically about the chapel and revealed a detailed knowledge of its design and construction, and the many Old and New Testament scenes portrayed in the stained glass. The interviewer expressed his surprise that the atheistic Miller was excited and moved by something that is so explicitly religious. Miller's response was to say that you don't have to believe in the story to be moved by its beauty and its power.

There is something very modern about Miller's reaction to Christianity, in his respectful appreciation of what could be called the aesthetic and emotional qualities of the Biblical story, while maintaining an air of well-mannered superiority over the question of belief. Yes, we can be moved by the drama that reaches its climax in Jesus Christ, just as we might be moved by the music and poetry of a great opera, but don't forget, at the end of the day it's just a story. Other ways of looking at the world are much more reliable.

Around the time that Miller was at his peak of artistic creativity and fame another person was contemplating the Christian story while in another building constructed mostly of stone, but with somewhat less of the architectural and aesthetic panache of King's College Chapel. The building was part of a labour camp (gulag) in the republic of Mordovia in Soviet Russia. Irina Ratushinskaya, a young poet, was held in the bare, stone built, solitary confinement cell in the high security heart of that camp because her poetry, which celebrated the beauty of nature, and the power of the Christian story to bring light and understanding into a dark and confusing world, was considered by the Soviet authorities to be 'anti-state' and subversive. Winter temperatures in her un-heated cell sometimes fell to -40 C. Deprived of paper and pen by prison orders she resorted to writing her poems by scratching them with a spent match on a bar of soap. Once written and committed to memory she erased them from the soap in case the guards discovered them. Sometime later they were smuggled out of prison having been written on cigarette paper by fellow inmates. Eventually reaching the West they, along with accounts of Irina's story, were published. She was released in 1986 and died of cancer, aged 63, in 2017.

Irina Ratushinskaya used her poetry to give expression to the way in which Christian faith, in her experience, offers a vision of beauty and truth that stands in direct opposition to not only the atheistic ideology of Soviet communism, but also the dead-end ideologies of modern materialism, individualism and resurgent pantheism that so afflict the West. Like thousands of people before and after her, Irina could be said to be an example of someone demonstrating the truth of the motto attributed to the mediaeval theologian St Anselm of Canterbury: 'faith seeking understanding'. That is to say, entering into faith in the triune God is not to be conceived as an arrival at a comforting destination but as a starting out on a journey of discovery and understanding. This book is an attempt to place the quest for understanding that the Christian journey of life involves ('Making Sense...') in the context of alternative and competing accounts of human experience and destiny, accounts which form the backdrop to modern life, especially those which are shaped by ideas and presuppositions encountered in contemporary Western culture. It is, to some extent, a dialogue with those alternative accounts, from a Christian perspective.

I have chosen four subject areas, four aspects of life (Time, Nature, Language and Person), which help to define what sort of world we inhabit, and the sort of challenges all people face. They do not constitute an exhaustive mapping of the territory, but they do seem to me to be strong candidates for inclusion in any reflective exercise on the mystery of living.

Rudyard Kipling's famous (perhaps infamous) take on time – 'If you can fill the unforgiving minute with 60 seconds worth of distance run, yours is the Earth and everything in it...' expresses something of the ambivalence we feel about it. It is both a threat ('unforgiving'), and an opportunity ('yours is the Earth... 'etc). Any serious consideration of time as a subject must involve some reflection on the facts of birth and death, boredom and anticipation, regret and hope, pessimism and optimism, history and the 'end of history'. We refer to a death that is unexpected or premature as 'untimely'. A person whose death forms a kind of satisfying closure of a long and fruitful life is sometimes described as having been 'full of years'. Wherever we turn, time is present. The journalist James Marriot has written about the mood of pessimism that afflicts many contemporary young people living in the apparently prosperous and liberal West as they react to the difficulties that colour their present and their future:

'Pessimism is a leitmotif of our age, a plangent minor chord sounding through our culture and politics. You can follow its echoes through the nihilism of online humour; the moody, claustrophobic disaffection of bedroom pop; the boom in dystopian fiction. Or through the arrival of anti-natalist ("birth strike") movements into the cultural mainstream; the fascination with the most cinematically apocalyptic prophecies of climate change.
The mood is measurable: in the rise of emotional disorders such as anxiety and depression; in the surveys that repeatedly report on the political and financial pessimism of the youngest generations. *(James Marriot, 'The Times', 3.8.22)*

The Christian contention is that time is part of what God has brought into being. Therefore, it must, more than anything else, be thought of as 'gift'. In what sense it is 'gift' is part of the account of 'Time' that we have tried to sketch out.

Some of the content of chapter 2 ('Nature') relates to the hot topic of the threat to our physical environment from human activity. A sub-heading for the chapter might have been 'Carbon, Creation and Christ', or even 'Footprint, Fabrication and Fulfilment'. The reason why only some of the content of the chapter relates directly to this aspect of 'Nature' is that before any discussion of the climate emergency can take place from a Christian perspective, some account must be attempted of the much wider and deeper convictions that Christian belief has concerning creation itself – its beginnings and its ultimate destiny especially. It is unfortunate that the contributions made by most church leaders to the debate about the climate emergency do little more than echo the sentiments expressed in the media and society at large, sentiments which any 'right thinking' but secular, or non-religious, person would express. This is unfortunate, given that interest in the 'spiritual' dimension of life, even if unorthodox in detail, is as evident as it has ever been in our apparently materialistic culture. The truth of the matter is that the Christian view of creation is rich in resources with which to approach the current crisis. Our chapter on 'Nature' is an attempt to mine some of those resources.

In the dramatic encounter on Mt Carmel between the prophet Elijah and the prophets of Baal, designed by Elijah to be a proof of the reality of the God of Israel and the unreality of Baal, Elijah taunts his opponents as they attempt to stir their god to action:

'At noon Elijah mocked them, saying, 'Cry aloud! Surely he is a god; either he is meditating, or he has wandered away, or he is on a journey, or perhaps he is asleep and must be awakened.' [28] Then they cried aloud and, as was their custom, they cut themselves with swords and lances until the blood gushed out over them. [29] As midday passed, they raved on until the time of the offering of the oblation, but there was no voice, no answer, and no response.' *(1 Kings 18: 27 – 29)*

No voice, no answer, no response. The silence of the false god is equated with impotence. By contrast, the God of Israel can be known, and is powerfully real, because he is the God who speaks. Then God *said* 'Let there be light.' *(Genesis 1:3)* Therefore words, the raw material of language, are important. Indeed, all that Christian belief says about anything finds its way back, sooner or later, to the God who makes himself known in the Word *(John 1: 1)*. Our chapter on 'Language' is an attempt to place our understanding of the function of words in the context of our knowledge of God who has spoken through his Word, who is Jesus Christ. It is also, to some extent, a plea on behalf of poetry and its capacity to penetrate more deeply than prose can into the meanings of things. Theology, and even some sermons(!), can be dry and prosaic. Part of our discussion revolves around the very unlikeliness of doing justice to the subject of God by the employment of speech. Yet the instinct to give verbal expression to vistas opened up by prayer, Scriptural study and experience is an undeniable part of our humanity. Poetry can be our most potent instrument in satisfying the instinct to say something truthful about God himself, without descending into trite formulae or over-confident simplifications. The poet Emily Dickinson makes this point with characteristic and deceptive simplicity:

Tell all the Truth but tell it slant –
Success in Circuit lies
Too bright for our infirm Delight
The Truth's superb surprise

As Lightning to the Children eased
With explanation kind
The Truth must dazzle gradually
Or every man be blind -

Competing theories about the realities of time, nature and language abound. We have made reference to a few of them in this preface, and to many more in the chapters themselves. Those competing theories are expressed in all sorts of ways and with considerable confidence. But they seem like quaint sideshows of only passing interest when compared to the bear-pit controversies surrounding the subject of 'Person' in contemporary life. Much of our discussion focuses on how our understanding of the notion of personhood is influenced by our culture's fascination, one might even say infatuation, with the self. Consciousness of self is very obviously an important part of our understanding of the person because the closest example of person with which we are familiar is our own self. Just how much the self has forced its way into the foreground of the landscape of modern Western culture is perceptively described by the well-respected journalist Matthew Syed:

> The verb "to share" has undergone a subtle but intriguing transformation. For most of my lifetime the concept was "other-directed": as one dictionary definition put it, to share is "to give some of (what one has) to someone else". Over the past few decades, however, the verb has taken on a new, inner-directed meaning, a point noted by the sociologist Robert Putnam in his book *The Upswing: How America Came Together a Century Ago and How We Can Do It Again*. The Merriam-Webster dictionary puts it this way: to share is "to talk about one's thoughts, feelings or experiences with others".
>
> I mention this because it hints at a deeper transformation in the way that people — particularly in the West — engage with the world. For most of the period since the scientific revolution, the emphasis was on external reality: measuring, engaging and transforming things to solve collective problems. We had shared empirical standards and objective conceptions of truth, ideals that sat behind the transformation in economics and technology that created the modern world.
>
> Over the past half-century, though, there has been what we might call an "inward turn". Our focus has shifted from the outer world to the inner self; from external reality to subjective feelings. This can be seen in many areas, not least the explosion in the sales of self-help books in the 1970s and 1980s and the rise of the self-esteem movement in education during the same period. More recently, we have seen a transformation in

photographic behaviour. At one point we took photos to remember events or vistas. Now we take "selfies": apparently no scene is considered worthy unless we are in it. *(Matthew Syed, 'The Times', 26.11.22)*

I had already sketched out the outline of the ideas I wanted to explore in the chapter on 'Person' before I came across this article. Reading it confirmed to me that I was not wrong in structuring the discussion around the concepts of 'the self' and of 'freedom'.

It is often pointed out that stained glass only 'works' when you look at it from the inside of the building it is part of, so that the sunlight can shine through it from the outside giving life to the colour which from the outside just looks dark and dull. I am not the first person to treat this appreciation as a metaphor for Christian faith. For most Christians thinking deeply about their faith and how it 'works' is an exercise that they find themselves engaging in in the space that opens up beyond the beginnings of their faith journey (from inside the chapel), especially as the presence of Christ, by the Spirit, throws new light on old problems and previously unencountered challenges. The intellectual pathway to faith, in which the seeker assesses and successively rejects varying philosophical or religious traditions until in the end Christianity is left standing alone, is a road less, even rarely, travelled. For most of us it is more like waking up in an unfamiliar and slightly exotic palace. The bed is comfortable, and the coffee is out of this world, and there are intriguing sounds coming from other wings of the palace, and from the estate in which it is located, which are impossible to ignore, some of them from the many other guests, both recently, and long since, arrived. In the end the corridors and interconnections leading to further discovery prove to be so multifarious that it is impossible for any single person to take it all in. As the discovery unfolds so does the reality and personality of the Host whose home it is.

In the course of our reflections on Time, Nature, Language and Person we will attend to what some of the great Christian thinkers of the past have said about Christian belief. Among them are St Anselm of Canterbury (11th century AD) and St Augustine (4/5th century AD). Anselm is well known for a saying that is a development of an Augustinian idea which expresses the necessary nature of intellectual enquiry if it hopes to make contact with the truth. It takes the following form: *'credo ut intellegam'* ('I believe in order to understand'). That is a very pertinent summary of the stained-glass analogy; that understanding is the product of, not the pre-condition for, faith.

Where I have quoted other authors I have referenced the source in the text itself for the sake of convenience, using just the author's name, the title of the source, and the date where possible. This is an abbreviation of the full academic style of referencing. Placing the information in the text itself removes the tiresome necessity of constantly having to look to the end of a chapter, or of the book, to follow up the source. I should also say that much of what I have written is not original, in the sense that I am not the person who first thought of the ideas I am writing about. I have used my own words to describe those ideas, and I have arranged and 'dressed them up' in ways which, I hope, are accessible, authentic, and perhaps even intriguing, especially in the context of contemporary debates. But many of the ideas can be found in other places, especially in the writings of those who are far wiser than I am. Amongst those writers are two theologians from whom I have borrowed liberally. Here and there I have referenced them formally, but their influence goes beyond those specific references, forming a kind of basic structure within much of what I have tried to build. It was Prof Colin Gunton, sometime Professor of Christian Doctrine at King's College London (Univ of London), who first pointed me in the direction of Irenaeus as perhaps the greatest of the early Christian thinkers, and who has done so much to revive interest in both the academy and the church in the doctrine of the Trinity. The other great influence on my theological thinking has been Prof John Webster (successively, Lady Margaret Professor of Divinity, Oxford, Chair of Systematic Theology, Univ of Aberdeen, and Chair of Divinity, Univ of St Andrews), who, like Colin Gunton, died tragically early, in his 60s. John Webster's emphasis on the importance of attending to Scripture's witness to God *as he is in himself* stands in contrast to many who would rather rush straight to, and stay within, the accounts of God's actions in the world. Reading John Webster is like watching a master craftsman deconstruct and then put back together again an exquisitely beautiful piece of furniture, whose quality you suspected, but are now seeing in all its intricate detail and glory.

When referencing or quoting from the Bible I have used the New Revised Standard Version (Anglicized) most of the time. Here and there I have used the King James Version because of its familiarity or poetic impact.

My thanks are due to Mr Stephen Anderson who read through the text and offered a number of very helpful corrections and suggestions. Any remaining shortcomings are entirely my responsibility.

Time

'Goldfinger' *(dir. Hamilton, 1964)* is perhaps the most iconic of all the Bond films in which, in the eyes of many film fans, Sean Connery establishes himself as the definitive Bond. The climax of the film unfolds somewhat formulaically – a race against time, in which Bond must try and work out how to deactivate the timer on the detonator of a nuclear bomb primed to explode inside Fort Knox, while being hand-cuffed to it.

The climactic scene is punctuated by occasional views of the counter on the device ticking down second by second. At the beginning of the scene the counter shows 58 seconds to go. Thirty seconds of action take place until the next glance at the counter, in which we see that there are now, apparently, 48 seconds to go...

No doubt the director wanted to squeeze into that final scene as much tension-infused action as he could; in fact, three times as much as would in reality be possible if the timer is to be believed! This disjunction between perception and reality in that Goldfinger scene is actually the wrong way round when compared to real life. Our perception of time is indeed somewhat elastic, depending upon what sort of thing we are doing. If what we are doing is important (e.g. defusing a nuclear bomb while the timer counts down) or enjoyable, time tends to speed up. There doesn't seem to be as much of it at our disposal as we would like. If what we are doing is routine or boring time seems to slow down.

Days, hours, minutes and seconds are the units that describe time's passing, and they are simply the calibration that measures the turning of the earth on its axis. That is time looked at as something that is a constant (notwithstanding

Einstein's discovery of the actual flexibility of time in certain contexts); something that is simply what it is, an objective reality. But as we have seen, our perception of it is anything but constant. Indeed, it seems to be rather elastic. We could call this the subjective reality of time.

The novelist and Christian apologist Dorothy L Sayers alerted us to the challenges of thought about Time:

'Time is a difficult subject for thought, because in a sense we know too much about it. .... all conscious thought is a process in time; so that to think consciously about Time is like trying to use a foot-rule to measure its own length.' ('Creed or Chaos? and other essays', Dorothy L Sayers, p 16)

The great thinkers of the past were often drawn to say something about time and what it says about the kind of world we are part of. St Augustine invested much intellectual energy in the pursuit of a satisfactory explanation of time as part of the created order of things ('*City of God*' *ch XI*). Among the many things he said about time is that it came into being with creation (i.e. time did not exist before creation). That there is no serious dissent from this assertion, even now, is indicated by the common currency of a term like 'space/time continuum' in popular cosmology. But Augustine felt himself to be less confident when dealing with our perception of time, especially the enigma, as he saw it, of the present, an experience or entity that he found impossible to pin down because of its 'passingness'. Describing the present as ever vanishing, is a way of trying to capture its elusiveness, and as the defining characteristic of our apprehension of time Augustine put the eggs of his conclusion firmly in the basket labelled 'subjective' (as opposed to the one labelled 'objective').

Underlying his varied, and to some extent, anxiety-laden musings was his conviction that the main product of time was change and decay, or that change and decay were the chief indicators of the reality of time. In this respect he was a conventional thinker of the ancient world in that he accepted Plato's dualistic world view, in which the eternal is constant and unchanging, while the realm of the physical or material, the world we inhabit, is temporal, and therefore in some sense inferior, unreal, destined to pass away. Plato's solution to the problem of the fleetingness and therefore the depressing pointlessness of our material world, which is presented to us through our senses, was to posit the existence of eternal Forms of those things that we see in our world, and which together make up our world. The actual examples in our experience will vanish, because they decay and eventually cease to exist, but, according to his concept of the Forms, they are mere copies of their original, essential and eternal selves in the realm (the eternal) which does not decay and die, and which therefore is timeless.

Plato famously described time as 'the moving image of eternity'. In other words, because time, as far as he was concerned, was the defining characteristic of the material order, and because it led inexorably to decay and non-existence, it meant that in our quest to discover ultimate reality we must look to the eternal, which, by definition, must be unchanging, timeless and therefore reliable. This material order offers hints and suggestions (moving images) regarding reality, but that is only because such hints are shadows of their eternal counterparts, the Forms. Clearly this established a very distinct hierarchy in the enterprise of acquiring reliable knowledge of anything, which was that the eternal in its fixed unchangingness is superior to the time bound world of change and decay.

This all seems somewhat abstruse, theoretical, and idealistic to us who are used to a very different paradigm of knowledge, that provided by science and its explanatory success in its application to the material order. But the Platonic residue still muddies the waters of even our modern and post-modern notions of knowledge, understanding and reality.

This Platonic bias or instinct is very evident in the matter of how the Christian account of God's dealings with creation through his Son are perceived or discussed, or in fact in many cases rejected. If it is taken that God's natural habitat (so to speak) is the eternal, Platonic assumptions tend to fix Him there and make any proposal that He has in fact entered the realm of time in all its change, decay, and unreliability absurd, or even impossible. This sort of assumption means that the Christian assertion, that in Jesus of Nazareth God was indeed present in time and space, is reinterpreted such that Jesus becomes simply an example, probably the best example, of how a man should live in an ethically heroic way, exemplifying that very modern category of discernment known as 'values'.

So, rather than allowing for the possibility that God may not in fact be thwarted by the apparently watertight boundary between eternity and space/time, Christ (it is usually 'Christ' rather than 'Jesus Christ' – sometimes an example of the downgrading of the physical particularity) is presented as a representation of ideals and values, as opposed to being the story of an actual man who lived, suffered, was crucified, died, was buried and then raised to life. This is why in most discussions about God in the modern and postmodern era God is conceived by agnostic participants deistically – hardly more than an impersonal concept, useful for arguments about things like First Causes; a kind of minimalist allowance towards the idea of agency as an explanation of why there is anything at all.

In other words the Christian account of God and his actions as described in the New Testament, and especially the Gospels, is made subject to an already existing conviction about what it is possible for God to do, or in fact, what it is not possible for Him to do. It is much easier to treat Jesus of Nazareth as an exemplar of certain values, an inspiration for a certain style of living, entered into as a process of self-improvement inspired by a very good man's example, because that programme of interpretation and response allows the human subject to retain control of how they live and what they do. Attending to Christ and taking from him what seems good becomes a kind of spiritual shopping trip – a bit of charity from here, a bit of humility from there.

An example of how Jesus Christ/Jesus of Nazareth can be reduced to Christ the purveyor of values was seen a few years ago in a British Religious Studies syllabus for 16-year-olds. Just one exam board (of the many) offered a paper requiring engagement with the Bible. This was in fact a study of the Gospel of Luke. At least, that was how it was described in the course rubric. Closer examination revealed that it was actually a study of a few Lucan extracts, mainly those that deal with Jesus' teaching on wealth and poverty (the parable about the man who felt the need to build bigger barns to store all his wealth), racial prejudice (the Good Samaritan) and the oppressed and marginalized of society (women, lepers, tax collectors, etc). In other words, it was the story of Jesus stripped down to just those parts that fit with the 'values' requirement as contained in the deeper rationale governing the inclusion of Religious Studies as a subject fit for study at school.

All those themes are entirely worthy of course, but by making no reference to the nativity, miracles, prayer, Jesus' arrest, trial, crucifixion and resurrection it was a bit like going out to a restaurant for a full-scale traditional Christmas lunch, only to find yourself served with one sprout, one potato and one baby carrot.

Elevating or privileging the eternal over the temporal, and therefore prioritizing idealism over deduction based on observation, has been the distinctive characteristic of philosophical speculation in the centuries since Plato right up to the Enlightenment and the dawning of what we might call the scientific era. During those long years time suffered the humiliation of being a kind of curse, the disease for which there was no cure. But with the arrival of experimental science and the throwing off of old religious certainties time, or temporality, gradually became not so much a curse as a blessing, or at least something to be no longer relegated but placed in the driving seat. The Enlightenment's most famous philosopher, Immanuel Kant, was no less a philosopher of idealism than Plato and the ancients. It's just that he reversed the order of things so that his idealism related not to the eternal realm but to the temporal. Eternity used to be lord of the household and the temporal world a mere servant. Now the roles were reversed. Discussing the nature of space and time he posed some rhetorical questions for his readers to consider:

> 'What then are space and time? Are they real existences? Are they only determinations of relations of things, yet such as would belong to things even if they were not intuited? Or are space and time such that they belong only to the form of intuition, and therefore to the subjective constitution of our mind, apart from which they could not be ascribed to anything whatsoever?' *(Immanuel Kant, 'Critique of Pure Reason' p68)*

The answer to the final question in this extract is clearly supposed to be 'Yes'. Yes, time, and even space, are merely mental constructs designed to allow us to marshal our experiences of the world 'out there' in ways that enable us to make sense of them. Their objective reality, whatever that might be, is subordinated to our mind's perception of them. Not only is eternity's transcendence disposed of but even the 'out there-ness' of our world is downgraded so that the intimacy and immediacy of our own thinking is now where it's at. Since for Kant time was the medium in which we experience the world through the exercise of our minds, time became, in effect, the only context in which we might know anything. It can never be bypassed so it must be in control of everything. The scullery maid was now installed as the lady of the manor. As Colin Gunton puts it: 'Plato went beyond time into a negative eternity; Kant beyond into a godlike mind.' *(Colin Gunton, 'Yesterday and Today', p107)*

In taking time to think about time in this way we can see something of the scale of the challenge that Christian apologetics faces when contesting the field of ideas through which some account of how things are can be essayed. In the history of ideas, the realms of eternity and temporality have been presented, on the whole, as competing alternatives. God is either transcendentally other, remote, and suitably located in the timeless perfection of eternity, or we are godlike in our habitation of the temporal which is, apparently, the sum total of what may be experienced and known. To suggest that eternity and space/time represent together the arena in which God chooses to have his being and express his creating is to highlight just how radical the Christian account is.

If it is the case that God graces time with his presence through indwelling his creation in the life of his Son, time is raised to a level of significance not seen in alternative world views, but without being divinized along Kantian lines. It is a servant still, but a servant without whom the master and his estate cannot achieve their ultimate purposes. The servant enjoys an honoured utility.

It is no accident, therefore, that the Biblical account of creation in Genesis 1 presents time as the stage on which the drama of creation's unfolding plays out. Creation, therefore, is the kind of thing which needs sequence, succession, becoming. Time is the medium in which God's providential ordering, redeeming, and perfecting exist. The story of creation as told in Genesis 1 is punctuated by a very significant commentary which chimes like a refrain through the account: 'And God saw that it was good'. 'Good', in this context, in fact means 'good for' — something that is entirely appropriate as the means to its end. Therefore time, being 'good for' is not, before the Fall, a threat, or a puzzle, or a problem, but a gift and an enabling.

It is hardly surprising therefore that the story told in the Bible, which starts 'in the beginning' and ends with a poetic portrayal of creation's eventual perfecting is exactly that – a story, and not a set of philosophical propositions, or a list of ethical imperatives, or a kaleidoscope of heroic deeds undertaken by mythical or semi-divine characters in an imaginary world. It tells of particular individuals and their actions undertaken in the unfolding story, in time, of a particular nation, culminating in the actions of the man in whom God's own being was present, who was 'crucified under Pontius Pilate', which is to say, at a particular time and in a particular place.

Time, then, from the biblical perspective, gives room for things to happen in sequence as the enterprise of creation makes its way from its beginnings to its fulfillment. One less than serious aphorism relating to time is the suggestion that God invented time so that everything doesn't have to happen all at once. But the biblical testimony to God's creating and redeeming engagement with what he has brought into being is not simply that a space is created for things to happen, one by one, so to speak, as if merely happening was enough, in which no event was more significant than any other event. What characterizes the unfolding story of creation and its redeeming through the history of a certain people, climaxing in the story of a particular Person from among those people, is that it moves forward towards the fulfillment of its story according to the purpose embedded in it. The story is not a collection of unconnected personal histories in which each life plays out as a self-contained cameo from which certain lessons might be drawn regarding how a person might live. This means that the church, the body of people who are called by God to be conformed to his Son, who is with them by his Spirit, finds itself at the centre of a story whose ending, although hidden in the future, and therefore as yet unseen, is assured by the recreating reality of the resurrection of Jesus, which event, although fixed in our past, establishes the certainty of the fulfillment of God's purpose in due time.

Here is a concept in which time's uni-directionality towards disappointment, decay and death becomes transformed from the dead end of philosophical speculation, and of the universal shadow of our mortality, to a vivified trajectory of hope as the historical event of the resurrection bursts out of the past so that it can transform our present and future. It is no longer a question of time being merely fixed or flexible depending on whether you lean towards objective or subjective. Redeemed time is now a gifted unfolding, whose beginnings and promise are fueled towards their consummation by a transformation undertaken within it by the game changer to end all game changers, the resurrection of Jesus Christ.

The Christian story is therefore a story that is pregnant with purpose. What God brought into being, whose progressive becoming he enables, will be completed, and that completion will display what is his intention in creating when creation praises the One in whom it has its being. 'At the name of Jesus every knee shall bow in heaven and on earth and under the earth' *(Philippians 2:10)*. Or, as Dante put it in his evocation of the Beatific Vision; the sight of the ecstatic, dazzling, overwhelming immediacy of the 'Love that moves the sun and other stars.' *('The Divine Comedy', Paradiso, XXXIII)*

It is worth dwelling a little on the idea of purpose as we have started to acknowledge it in our thinking about the unfolding of creation's story in time. We know from ordinary human experience that purpose fortifies the activities we engage in, encouraging us to overcome difficulties as our projects move from conception to completion. We set our hands to the plough in order to achieve a specific end. But purpose is not limited only to certain sorts of activity in which components are combined mechanically in order to achieve a function or produce utility.

The philosopher Mary Midgley has reminded us that those activities which seem to us to be the most fulfilling and creative have an inbuilt purpose that transcends mere utility. In a discussion of teleology (the explanation of things based on their purpose) and time she says this:

'...the first notes of a song are not a means to its cadence, nor the first ten years of a friendship a means to its final end. The essential teleological question is not 'what later thing is this leading to?' It is, more widely, 'what is this for, and what is the point of it?'....Acts like singing are intentional – they are done 'on purpose'- but not for the sake of producing consequences. The essential relation involved is not of earlier to later time. It is that of part to whole.' *(Mary Midgley, 'Science as Salvation', p10)*

It is interesting that she takes singing as an example of something that shows us a deeper dimension of the idea of purpose than mere utility. In fact, as we are well aware, music and time have a very close relationship with each other, not just in the way in which time functions as a regulatory framework within its own structures (as in 4/4 time, or 6/8 time etc) but also in the way in which music needs time to be what it is.

The musicologist Victor Zuckerkandl presented a powerful argument in favour of music's ability to indicate that time is neither disqualified from bearing reality (Plato) nor the jailer who imprisons everything inside our minds (Kant). When we hear music we experience something that comes to us from a source outside of ourselves, and in a form that takes time to reach completion. This suggests very strongly that the relationship between time and reality is not one of illusion or futility but of cooperation and articulation. Music is a universal feature of human culture and infinitely capable of giving expression to the full range of experiences that human beings undergo. It offers therefore a very significant check to those who still maintain that temporality makes our longing for knowledge of the fully real an unrealizable fantasy.

Looking into the apparent mystery of the fleetingness of the present moment, that feature of time that so troubled Augustine, Zuckerkandl proposes that

'....The present of musical experience is not the dividing point that eternally separates past and future; it is the stage upon which, for every ear, the drama of the being of time is played – the ceaseless storing of itself and anticipating itself which is never repeated, which is every instant new.'
(Victor Zuckerkandl, 'Sound and Symbol', p225)

Philosophers, and some theologians have wanted to present to us on the one hand the timeless, or on the other the transient, as a choice that we must make if we are going to have any idea about the world, ourselves, and the ultimate realities that govern how things are. But music shows us that the choice between the timeless and the transient (or temporal) is an oversimplification at best and a false dichotomy at worst. One of Zuckerkandl's summaries of what music can teach us about time is his comment that 'Music is temporal art in the special sense that in time it reveals itself to experience.' *(Victor Zuckerkandl,'Sound and Symbol' p 200)*

We are very familiar with how music forms such a central part in the act of worship in most religious traditions, and especially so in Christianity. You don't have to be a philosopher or an intellectual to know that in hearing the best music time and eternity can seem to be fused into a creative and limitless experience in which depths of perception and intimations of knowing transcend our mundane thought processes. The connection between music and apprehensions of the eternal may well amount to more than mere analogy.

In his fascinating study of the workings of the human brain Iain McGilchrist, the psychiatrist, neuroscientist, and literary critic, draws our attention to the fact that music is 'forever unfolding in time, a thing that is ever changing, never static or fixed, constantly evolving, with the subtle pulse of a living thing.' *(Iain McGilchrist, 'The Master and his Emissary', p73)* He unpacks some of the detail of how music works by describing music as being, essentially, relational. That is to say, music takes its form not just from the notes that go to make up the song, minuet or symphony, but by the combination of the notes with everything else that gives those notes their context – especially the silences and pauses that exist between them, giving rise to features such as rhythm, articulation, phrasing and meaning itself. Neither the notes, nor the silences, are by themselves, 'music'. It is their *relatedness in time* that allows music to come into being. In one of their famous Christmas Shows on British television in the 1970s the comedy duo

Morecambe and Wise performed a sketch with Andre Previn who was, at the time, the conductor of the London Symphony Orchestra. (For Morecambe and Wise fans the existence of this sketch on YouTube is, by itself, enough justification for the very existence of that well-known video platform.) Eric Morecambe, in a piece of pure music hall comedy, took the part of guest soloist in a performance of Grieg's 1st piano concerto. There ensued a perfectly simple and eternally hilarious demonstration of how notes by themselves are only part of the story. The orchestra played the opening introductory bars teeing up Morecambe for his big dramatic entry – at which point he plonks out a simple nursery rhyme tune. The horrified Previn accuses him from his rostrum vantage point: 'You are playing all the wrong notes!' With immaculate comic timing Morecambe explains 'I'm playing all the right notes. But not necessarily in the right order.'

Perhaps few poets have been as accomplished as George Herbert in adopting music as the 'costume' in which his meaning comes to us. His poem entitled 'Easter' contains the following lines:

Awake, my lute, and struggle for thy part

                With all thy art.

The crosse taught all wood to resound his name,

                Who bore the same.

His stretched sinews taught all strings, what key

Is best to celebrate this most high day.

Consort both heart and lute, and twist a song

                        Pleasant and long:

Or since all musick is but three parts vied

                        And multiplied;

O let thy blessed Spirit bear a part,

And make up our defects with his sweet art.

Vaughan Williams' setting of this poem in his 'Five Mystical Songs' effects a profoundly moving coming together of meaning and form; Herbert's words given musical clothing befitting their heavenly theme.

Music therefore has much to show us about how reality may be perceived and especially how some historically significant ideas about time and eternity (Augustine, Kant etc) are in fact cul-de-sacs rather than highways to the truth. Music's truth-bearing goes beyond the poetic and emotional into the realms of philosophy, teleology, and theology. It also has something to show us regarding the role that our senses have in our encounters with meaning and truth.

We are very used, especially in the Western world, to the use of sight as the primary, or most commonly deployed, sense when it comes to the business of investigation and discernment. The microscope and the telescope between them sum up the dominance of the eye as the organ that we must use, apparently, in the enterprise of discovery. Even language itself reflects this tendency. When we want to know if someone has understood something we ask them 'Do you see?' Commercial enterprises like to publish their mission statements in which they present to the world their best selves. Invariably such documents contain a liberal sprinkling of the word 'vision' ('Our vision is to make a positive difference to the communities that we are part of....etc.'). The sub-title of this book falls into the same metaphor trap ('....through the *lens* of Christian belief') such is the ubiquity and apparent unavoidability of this way of thinking.

In the light of this, music stands as a reminder that sight alone is insufficient as a faculty through which we can know the truth of things. Indeed, from the Christian perspective sight comes a very distant second to hearing as the primary sense through which we come to know the truth, especially the truth about ourselves. The prophets of Israel were charged not with constructing visible, physical representations of God but with the responsibility of speaking the word of God that it might be heard. The people heard God's words of judgement and grace. There was nothing for them to see – indeed no-one could see God and live *(Exodus 33:20)*. As people of the word they had a calling (not a vision) to fulfil. It was the heathen who craved gods that could be seen. To give in to that same craving (as in the incident of the golden calf at Sinai while Moses was in God's presence at the summit of the mountain) was to abandon their calling, and therefore to choose death over the living word of God.

We are so used to the metaphor of sight as a way of describing how we come to the knowledge of things that questioning its validity seems to be like questioning whether breathing is the best way to gain access to oxygen. Attending to the biblical paradigm of hearing as the principle 'avenue of knowing' at least gives us pause for thought, and some warrant for thinking the unthinkable as far as the metaphor of sight is concerned. It is also important to recognise that challenging the dominance of the metaphor of sight is not confined just to the biblical witness. Michael Polanyi was a Hungarian practitioner, observer and philosopher of science working and writing in the mid-20th century. He questioned the effectiveness of the metaphor of sight as a way of understanding reality, recognizing that it tended to promise a false objectivity because of its detachment from that which is being contemplated. He suggested that picturing reality by means of the metaphor of sight (as opposed to other ways of understanding the act of knowing) was like being in an aircraft flying over a landscape below and looking down on it critically and apparently omnisciently. Consequently truths relating to reason and sense experience, especially in the enterprise of science, resulted in the privileging of such knowledge while down-grading or even ignoring forms of knowledge relating to morality, politics, aesthetics and theology. Hence the lop-sidedness in favour of science in modern understandings of the enterprise of knowing.

Polanyi proposed a different way of picturing how we gain authentic knowledge of the world and of ourselves, a way that complements the biblical paradigm of hearing. He suggested the metaphor of 'indwelling'. He used the picture of a blind man and his white stick as a way of imagining how we explore and come to a knowledge of reality. In the activity of feeling his way forward the man indwells his stick, in the sense that he comes to know what is actually out there in front of, but separate from, him through the instrument he is holding in his hand. He quite genuinely feels in his hand what is going on at the other end of the stick. The dentist uses her probe in the same way as she explores the topography of the cavity in her patient's tooth. Our mental concepts, and language itself, function as the stick or probe, so allowing us to come to a knowledge of what it is we are exploring, and to do so in ways that are open to the unexpected. Picturing the enterprise of knowing as indwelling also preserves and highlights its personal nature. As human beings we are fallible and our attempts to know things will always be only partially successful. But that does not invalidate the limited knowledge that we acquire. It simply functions as a stage on the way to greater and more complete knowledge as the openness of indwelling allows us to know and be known in the world as it is in its mystery and profundity. Polanyi took great pains to make clear, and demonstrate, that the metaphor of indwelling applies just as accurately to the scientific enterprise of knowing as it does to any other field of enquiry. From the Christian perspective this language of 'indwelling' reminds us of the Gospel of John and the metaphors used by the evangelist to describe God's presence in the Christian believer as 'dwelling' or 'abiding'.

And I will ask the Father, and he will give you another advocate to help you and be with you forever— the Spirit of truth. The world cannot accept him, because it neither sees him nor knows him. But you know him, for he lives with you and will be in you. *(John 14:16 – 17)*

Remain in me, as I also remain in you. No branch can bear fruit by itself; it must remain in the vine. Neither can you bear fruit unless you remain in me. *(John 15:4)*

We will pursue this important subject in more detail in chapter 3 ('Language').

Platonic and Kantian attitudes to time attempt to offer solutions to its being a problem, if problem it is. In considering these apparent solutions we have seen something of how the Christian gospel radically undermines their conclusions. But there is a further contribution from the Christian gospel to the debate about how we should think about time that we have not yet mentioned and that is the matter of hope.

Both the Platonic and the Kantian frameworks of understanding regarding time have a dauntingly severe feel to them. Plato's 'solution' seems to downgrade the temporal so that our existence becomes drained of real significance because it is in the eternal, apparently, that reality has its being. It is as if our past, present and future are playing out in what is, in effect, a sideshow. The main event is elsewhere. If this is the case, what are we to do with the impulse that is present in most of us which is the hope that our story might in fact have some substance, some purpose?

The Kantian view is equally intimidating because by locating everything within the temporal sphere alone we find that the burden of responsibility that it places on humanity is too great. Everything is up to us. But even a cursory glance at history indicates that we are incapable of building a 'New Jerusalem' ourselves. Indeed, we are experts at destroying rather than conserving or creating. Meanwhile the plaintive cry from the heart that pleads for harmony, peace, and a bright new dawn dissolves into the silent and unhearing void. If we cannot save ourselves our salvation must rely on something or someone else from outside this vale of tears, but if this order of which we are a part is all that there is, such hopes are doomed to disappointment.

In common discourse hope is understood as being something that human beings do, often against a backdrop of anguish, or pain, or thwarted ambition, or simply a desire to see things get better. There is much truth in this, at least from a straightforwardly human perspective. Hoping for the best is a universal and entirely normal response to the uncertainties and difficulties of life. It is, by definition, an attitude of mind that is oriented to the future, and in that respect it says something about our experience of time. It stands as a kind of psychological counterbalance to the troubling unknowability of the future.

The essential character of hope within the Christian worldview, as distinct from hope exercised from outside that worldview, is that it has its grounding in the faithfulness of God. That is to say, it is not a mind-set that is summoned from the inner resources of the person who hopes, having a rationale and a potential in accordance with the resilience and optimism of the one who hopes. Christian hope rests not on the abilities of the one who hopes, but on the utter faithfulness of God as it is seen in his actions in and for creation in the person of his Son. This is why the first letter of Paul to Timothy opens with the following statement or introduction:

'Paul, an apostle of Christ Jesus by the command of God our Saviour and of Christ Jesus our hope.' *(1 Tim 1:1)*

In speaking this way Paul reminds us of the principle that underlies our hoping when it takes place within Christian believing and living, which is that before it is an attitude of mind, or even the motive force behind some action undertaken, it is nothing less than the action of God in Jesus Christ himself. It is Jesus who defines what we mean by hope. Hope, in this perspective, has no meaning outside of the reality of Jesus through whom God has established creation and its perfecting. And because our fellowship with God through Jesus Christ is made possible by the activity of the Holy Spirit ('May the God of hope fill you with all joy and peace in believing, so that you may abound in hope by the power of the Holy Spirit.' *Romans 15:13*) our hoping is revealed to be a participation in the tri-unity of God's own life. This is true not only for hope, of course, but for all other attributes that flow from our incorporation in Christ through faith in him, especially, of course, faith itself, and love *(1 Cor 13:13)*.

Therefore hope as a human activity is transformed from being a somewhat forlorn attempt to colour the future with a tint of positivity, to an act of contemplation – contemplation of the triune God in his sovereign majesty, whose commitment to the perfecting of creation is seen in the gift of his Son, through whom all things have their being, and in whom all things must find their completing, by the outworking of his resurrection, and the 'fashioning of perfection' that is the distinctive work of the Holy Spirit in creation.

We are accustomed to thinking about the story of God's acts, in creation itself, and the calling into being of a particular people, and his immersion into the messy reality of creation in its need by his blessed Son, as the golden thread of our past; that which gives some sort of shape to the complexity and misery of human history, while we and our contemporaries press forward with that story in our wake, so to speak. But, as we have seen, hope is Jesus Christ; and the certainty of God's faithfulness towards his creation through the Son means that the most significant thing about the future is that it is destined to be perfected, to be conformed to the purpose that is inherent in the loving acts of God already seen. We do not stand precariously at the moving edge of time as the past slips behind us and the future laps at our feet as we peer into the unsettling darkness of the unknown which lies up ahead. Instead, we stand in the presence of One who is 'Alpha and Omega...who is, and who was, and who is to come, the Almighty.' *(Rev 1:8)*

If the final scenes of Goldfinger prompt us to reflect on the flexibility of time, other films and TV shows demonstrate the fascinating hold that time has on our imaginations. None, more so, perhaps, than 'Back to the Future' *(dir. Robert Zemeckis, 1985)*. The fascination in what might happen if we could travel backwards or forwards in time, with all the practical and philosophical conundrums that it would involve, gives us an insight into the grip that time has on us as a dimension that helps to define our being.

Any connection between 'Back to the Future' and Moses might seem at first sight to be somewhat tenuous. But the past and the future are very much in the frame at that seminal event of Moses' calling, his encounter with God at the Burning Bush. Moses had fled Egypt under a cloud of suspicion. To return there would have meant exposing himself to the consequences of his having killed an Egyptian taskmaster. But

God was now commissioning him to go back and lead his people out. It was not a matter of having the chance to change or divert the past, but of finding a new way forward to a path of both personal and national redemption. Daunted by the scale of a seemingly impossible, perhaps suicidal, mission, Moses seeks to know the true identity of the God of the Israelites' ancestors so that he can have something to say when his credentials are examined by the enslaved Israelites.

'I am who I am' comes the now well-known reply, as it is usually rendered in English *(Exodus 3:14)*. But the meaning of the Hebrew in question cannot be limited to a static sate of being as implied by 'I am who I am' with its apparently tautological tone. The Hebrew in question is the word *hayah* (in phonetic transliteration). In addition to referring to 'being' it also contains the idea of 'becoming'. In other words it contains a strong dynamic of movement in a forward direction, if we can so describe it. It is not so much future proofed as future embracing. God reassures Moses *(Ex 3: 12)* with a declaration not that he, God, merely is, as in the sense of essential being, but that he will 'become' with him in the perilous task that lies ahead. Not 'back to the future' but forward to the future in the presence of One who, knowing the chaos of the past, is able to make that past the starting point of an unthought of, and seemingly impossible, future. The divine name itself contains the affirmation of movement towards a purposed end, which, by implication, means that time is not an embarrassment to God, but has been woven into the underlying pattern of how things in fact are, and how he relates providentially to them.

Hope from the Christian perspective is, therefore, 'both prospective and retrospective. It is rooted in faith's trust in a *future* perfection which *has been* promised and secured.' *(John Webster, 'Confessing God', p196)*

It may well be that of all the ways in which an investigation into the attributes and experience of time might be attempted, approaching the matter through an exploration of the importance of hope is the most fruitful. In addition to being intimately related to the dimension of time as an example of human beings' experience of temporality (even to be in such desperate straits as to be without hope functions as an inverse affirmation of this) hope also points us towards our own role in the perfecting of creation. It has, therefore, a practical outworking or application, and is not merely a passive 'state of mind'. Hope signals the fact that all human history is the field of the triune God's economy of mercy – the enterprise of saving, enabling and perfecting that which is the object of God's love – the creation itself. Thus hope, Christianly understood, draws us into action which gives a particular Christ-like shape to the present in which it is carried out. This means that all acts of compassion and creativity undertaken in affirmation of those in need, and in celebration of the saving love of God in Christ, become the building blocks of the perfecting that the Holy Spirit makes it his joyful undertaking to complete. They become evidences of hope at work, because they arise from the enabling presence of Him who is himself hope, none other than Jesus Christ, crucified, risen, ascended, and now, by his Spirit, with his people.

Luther is purported to have said when asked what his reaction would be to the certain knowledge that the world would end tomorrow that he would 'Go out and plant an apple tree'. That has a remarkably contemporary feel, in relation to 'green' issues. But it is also a wonderful example of Christian hope issuing in practical action.

Rooting hope in the faithfulness of God revealed in the life, death, resurrection and ascension of his Son has the advantage of protecting us from a narrow conception of hope, limited only to the future, and especially the future coming of the Son. That this narrow conception of hope is relatively common is indicated by the many instances of religious sects built on the notion of the single issue of the 'end of the world' and Jesus' return. Many are the cases of such groups gathering at a particular place and time in order to be whisked away and out of the doom that will apparently befall the world. Mainstream churches do not tend to take things so far in their interpretation of the implications of the limit placed on time's duration by the fact that a story that has begun is bound also to have an ending, never mind the account of Jesus' ascension in Acts 1 within which his future return is announced *(Acts 1: 11)*. Hope must relate to the future, of course, but not in such a way that the future is isolated from the past and present, becoming a kind of special interest subject for those who see their salvation as being from the world (as opposed to in it) or as an excuse to indulge in exotic or literalistic interpretations of the Book of Revelation.

In an episode of the much-loved British sitcom Fawlty Towers, Basil Fawlty (played by John Cleese) takes aside his Spanish waiter Manuel (played by Andrew Sachs) to explain something to him. Manuel's English is less than perfect thus providing rich comedic possibilities in the encounter. Manuel finally gets what it is that Basil has been trying to explain after many hilarious excursions down blind alleys of incomprehension. In a 'light bulb' moment Manuel demonstrates his grasp of what he is expected to do in the hours that follow by declaring, with a radiant beam on his face, 'Event-u-ally!' Fawlty, not convinced that Manuel really understands the word he has just used waits for Manuel to elaborate. 'At the end', comes the rejoinder. Unlikely as it may seem that Fawlty Towers provides lessons in theology (as opposed to human frailty and comedy) it could be claimed that at least accidentally this scene reminds us that our experience of time is not open-ended. All of the component parts of our lives as they unfold are defined by beginnings and endings — be they personal projects like courses of study or projects at work, or tacit stratagems entered into by a hotel owner and his Spanish waiter, or our very lives themselves, bookended by our births and our deaths.

The author of the Book of Revelation (known as 'John') poured his considerable poetic and pastoral abilities into producing a kaleidoscopic representation of the theological background to the deep question of why God's justice seemed to be so greatly delayed. The members of the young churches to whom he wrote, in what we now call Asia Minor, were experiencing the reality of what Jesus himself had warned would be the case for those who followed him:

'Blessed are you when people hate you, and when they exclude you, revile you and defame you on account of the Son of Man.' *(Luke 6: 22)*

And for the recipients of John's letter (what we call The Book of Revelation) solidarity with their Lord, faithful testimony to him in word and deed, meant experiencing the same rejection and defamation that Jesus endured on the way to his execution, and for many of them, the same gory outcome – their martyrdom at the hands of the imperial authorities whose insistence on unquestioning allegiance from every citizen presented Christians with the starkest of choices: conform to those earthly powers, or pay with their lives for their allegiance to Christ. In the midst of this 'crisis of authority' in which those early Christians looked for signs of the victory of God over the demonic forces at loose in society, in which the authority of God seemed to be dismissively denied by the overweening political and military arrogance of Rome, their cry went up: 'How long O Lord, how long?'

'Sovereign Lord, holy and true, how long will it be before you judge and avenge our blood….?' *(Rev 6: 10)*

One way of describing the mistake that the Second Coming fanatics make with their regular retreats to a convenient hilltop in preparation for their whisking away to safety is that they focus on the End exclusively as an event rather than as a person i.e. the One who is the End, in the sense of his being the One in whom all things find their consummation or completion, the Alpha and the Omega. Their mistake is to think that salvation is salvation 'from', as opposed to salvation 'in and through'. When the persecuted Israelites Shadrach, Meshach and Abednego were thrown into the fiery furnace *(Daniel 3)* because of their refusal to obey Nebuchadnezzar's order God did not 'tele-transport' them into the heavenly realms milliseconds before they fell into the flames. His salvation took the form of his angelic presence with them *in the midst of* the flames.

For the members of those beleaguered churches to whom John wrote their vindication is assured, but only as they advance along the way that their Lord trod on his way to the cross. It is not that the prospect of martyrdom provides an opportunity for romantic indulgence in heroic self-sacrifice as a way of demonstrating extreme devotion to a fallen leader. That might be justifiable if the story of their leader ended with his fateful extinguishing on that Roman execution gibbet. The snuffing out of the beauty of his person and his life in that barbaric act might well draw forth acts of devoted imitation from fatalistic followers who were convinced that honour would be satisfied by their deaths. However, John reminds them that their Lord does not address them from the tearful depths of painful memories associated with a horrific and ultimately pointless death, but from the living immediacy of his majestic, triumphant, risen presence in their midst. That is why John starts his pastoral communication to them with a description of the One who addresses them as:

'...Jesus Christ, the faithful witness, the firstborn of the dead, and the ruler of the kings of the earth.' *(Rev 1:5)*

John prefaces this arresting and uplifting description of their Saviour with an equally startling and allusive description of God as 'him who is, and who was, and who is to come.' It echoes the answer given at the Burning Bush when Moses sought assurances about God's true identity. 'I am who I am', which, as we saw above, also carries the meaning of 'I will become who I will become.' John has no embarrassment in presenting God in terms that highlight God's engagement with and lordship over time. A few sentences later John repeats and expands this 'time laden' title by reporting God's authorial declaration:

'I am the Alpha and the Omega' says the Lord God, who is, and who was, and who is to come, the Almighty.' *(Rev 1: 8)*

Amidst such distinctive and remarkable language it is easy to miss the particular form that is used here to place God in relationship with time. If it were left to us to frame God in such terms we would instinctively place the tenses in time order – the One who was, who is, and is to come. Past, present and future, in the right order. But John records God's self-identification as He 'who is, and who was, and who is to come'.

To think of God as being 'in the past' or 'in the future' carries a temptation to see Him as being remote – a figure of historical curiosity on the one hand, or potential significance at some later date on the other. Yet, God is the God *who is*, in the here and now – or as George Caird puts it, the 'eternal present' *(G B Caird, 'The Revelation of St John the Divine', p16)*, in which all of the past and the future are embraced and incorporated. This is the reality of Christ's presence with his suffering people. He is with them because he is the present one – not just in the sense of spatial proximity, but also in the sense of the eternal present, the eternal *now*. St Augustine – eat your heart out!

As John puts it later in the first chapter of the Book of Revelation this Jesus who addresses his suffering people is the One who is 'in the midst of the lampstands' *(Rev 1:13)*, where the lampstands are John's poetic image for the seven churches to whom he is writing.

The explicit, deliberate acknowledgement of time in Christian thought as being not only affirmed by God's personal involvement with it in the Incarnation, but also taken up into a description of God's own being (as in Revelation 1, Exodus 3, and elsewhere) stands in dramatic contrast to philosophical attempts to make sense of time in the face of its elusiveness, and time's apparent threat to the hopes that humanity might have for some destiny that is not subject to its power to usher in darkness and death.

Nature

A few years ago there was a programme on British TV called something like 'Best Home Wins' that could be found in the slack backwaters of daytime programming, in which proud house owners showed other contestants, and the viewers at home of course, round their house and garden. The contestants then all voted on each-others' houses and gardens at the end of the show. No doubt the winner got a garden-centre voucher or something.

In a perfect illustration of Andy Warhol's aphorism about everyone in the modern world being famous for 15 minutes a contestant showed us round her house and garden – pointing out all the eco-friendly features, and the extent to which her dwelling and lifestyle were deeply attuned to the rhythms and resonances of the natural world. Nothing wrong with that.

The centrepiece of her back garden was a small to medium sized tree, which to my eye looked singularly unremarkable, but as far as she was concerned - and her voice took on a kind of hushed awe as she shared this with us – as far as she was concerned, the tree 'contained great wisdom, because it knows so much more than we do.' The programme did not mention where she lived, but I so much wanted it to be Braintree, a small town in Essex, England.

I don't think there is any doubt that this lady was leaning towards the looney side of the new fashion for 'connecting with the spiritual/natural' side of life – that is so much part of the Western mainstream now, especially in its pantheistic divinization of the natural world.

'Braintree' lady may represent the popular end of the spectrum that relates to the modern phenomenon of personalizing or even divinizing nature. But she has her more respectable counterparts at the literary end of that spectrum. The prolific and well respected author Richard Mabey who has been writing on things natural, flora and fauna mostly, for the last 40 years made the following comments in an article reflecting on the way in which public consciousness of the natural environment has developed over that period of time: 'What I have written most recently about plants celebrates their possession of agency, and maybe intelligence….. As we try to get closer to nature in our environmental crisis, wild organisms are becoming seen as partners, creative cultural subjects, not just objects.' (*Daily Telegraph, 8.10.19*). The 'clothing' is more respectable, but the ideas are at one with those expressed in that Braintree back garden.

Pointing out this tendency to personalize, even divinize, the natural world is not the same thing as saying that humanity does not need to take more seriously its conservational responsibilities towards the natural world. It is simply an attempt to highlight the limitations inherent in having an account of creation that looks no further than the imminent (i.e. its own structures of being) when seeking an ethic of environmental best practice. Christian belief approaches the subject not from the direction of the imminent, but from the transcendent. That which God has brought into being can only be fully understood from God's perspective, and that perspective is only accessible to humanity if God chooses to reveal it. The Christian claim is that God has indeed revealed it, through becoming part of his creation in the life, death, and resurrection of Jesus of Nazareth, through the activity of his Spirit, and by creation itself coming into being through the mediating activity of the Second Person of the Trinity and reaching its fulfilment in him. One less than impressive aspect of many pronouncements by church leaders on the hot subject of care for the environment is that too often they seem to be nothing more than echoes of what is already being said, and usually much more knowledgeably, by secular commentators. In the same way that an actual Rolling Stones concert is more compelling than that of a Rolling Stones tribute group playing their set on a Friday evening down the pub. We look in vain for contributions drawing on the immensely rich resources contained in full-blooded Christian believing which take us far beyond merely polite respect for something that we do not own, or anxious hand-wringing in the face of serious problems.

The extent to which the churches have bought into a secular approach to these problems can even result in not merely ignoring a distinctively Christian analysis but in suggesting that it should be replaced by something more contemporary. Recently a Swedish church issued the following statement on its Twitter account: 'For her defence of the environment……Greta Thunberg is the successor of Jesus Christ.' I am tempted to wonder what Greta Thunberg would make of Jesus' management of the environment when he stilled the storm *(Mark 4: 35 – 41)* or sent the Gadarene swine *(Mark 5: 1 – 20)* to their deaths. Would she have approved of his 'manipulation' of it? I suspect not. It is too easy to get the impression that the church's pronouncements on the subject are rather like Shakespeare turning up to a writing workshop that didn't get beyond 'how to write limericks'. He can join in, of course, but what about his achievements in writing *Hamlet, Lear* and *Macbeth*?

If we make our starting point in the discussion the proposal that what we call creation is the result of God's deciding and acting, a number of important (and very useful) principles flow from this.

The first is that, because creation belongs to God, its destiny must lie within what God has purposed to undertake, in and through what he has brought into being. This does not negate the important and vital role that humanity has in caring for the part of creation that is its home (the Earth), even when the motivation for that commitment arises from a secular worldview that is simply compassionate towards the natural order, and mindful of the kind of world we want our grandchildren to experience. But it does restore a sense of perspective. If creation is moving towards some sort of destiny that God has promised, our attempts to exercise proper care for creation will be carried out in the conviction that, in the end, his will cannot be thwarted because his sovereignty over creation as its creator, redeemer and perfecter is genuine. The tone of our caring will be not so much panicky anger but determined optimism. If we merely echo the secular account, we run the risk of implying that, in fact, God is not sovereign over what he has created and upholds, and if *we* don't do something creation will be destroyed.

Therefore 'doing something' is an outworking of a relationship that humanity has with its home under the providential enabling of its Creator, fulfilled in joyful obedience. This is part of what it means to say that humanity is commissioned by God to be carers of creation, or as Genesis 1:26 puts it, to exercise dominion over it.

Before moving on to the rich resources contained in orthodox Christian belief about God and that which is not God (what we call 'creation') it will be useful to examine more closely some of the implications of a purely secular approach to the natural order, the philosophy which underlies much contemporary thinking about humankind's predicament in a fragile and threatened world.

We have already noticed in our treatment of the subject of Time that what we call the modern (or contemporary) era is characterized by the remarkable success story of the rise of science and its power to explain how the natural world works, especially in the eighteenth century as the achievements of the Enlightenment took root. That story is, of course, ongoing because science never reaches a point where everything is completely explained or understood. The jump from religious or idealistic 'explanations' of things to explanations that arise from apparently dispassionate and objective study carried with it an implicit invitation to make the further jump of abandoning altogether the idea of God, or ideas based on prior philosophical convictions. The reactions within Western society to this sea-change were many and various, but they included the phenomenon of what came to be called Romanticism (or the Romantic era or movement) which emerged during the late eighteenth and early nineteenth century and took up a place alongside the march of science towards the confident simplicities of the Modern era, in which science seemed to have sealed its success as the universal provider of knowledge, and the justification for optimism and secular humanism. It is important to remember, of course, that those 'confident simplicities' relate especially to what is known as 'scientism' (rather than to science as such), which is the idea that scientific knowledge has made redundant every other kind of knowledge. Most scientists are not believers in scientism, but scientism does lurk under the surface of much popular discussion about God and creation.

Romanticism represented an attempt to recover something of the experience of awe and reverence in the face of nature and its glories and mysteries. At one level it resulted in simple artistic and aesthetic appreciation (e.g. Wordsworth, Delacroix etc), while at a deeper level it embraced a conviction that humanity was being called (or recalled) to a relationship with the natural order that would not only value that order for itself but would also lead to a more holistic understanding and experience of what it means to be human.

Jean-Jacques Rousseau (1712 – 1778) is often taken to be the father of Romanticism. His account of the human condition did not involve rejection of God so much as a reimagining of God according to his own terms. Of his many terse statements purporting to contain the essence of his ideas the following will suffice:

'I perceive God everywhere in his works. I sense Him in me; I see Him all around me.' *(Jean Jacques Rousseau, 'Emile: Or on Education', 1762)*

Taken with his wider philosophical vision in which man is placed at the centre, freed from the restraints of tradition and societal authority, we can see how enduring his perspective is. There is something very contemporary about his retention of the idea of God as a way of talking about the beauty, meaning and significance of the natural world, and also of the way in which God is 'internalized'. God, in this perspective, as well as leaning towards being the same thing as nature in its splendour and variety (i.e. pantheism), becomes also an affirming inner presence ('I sense Him in me'), something or someone who is not over and against me, or the one who is Other than me, and whose awe-full holiness would consume me were it not for his compassionate mercy, but who is essentially a version of me, or an aspect of my own self-consciousness. That being the case, this 'God' can never be the God who confronts me with my need for forgiveness and wholeness. He can only be to me much as my pet dog is to me – something that I control and deploy to my own ends.

Hymn writers have been stimulated by concerns about our despoilment of the natural order to challenge the churches to rediscover a sense of awe and responsibility in the face of the beauty and fragility of God's creation (e.g. 'Touch the earth lightly' by Shirley Erena Murray). No Harvest Festival service is complete without the singing of a hymn which invites an awareness of our guilt and our need for confession to the Creator of the world we inhabit, and that is as it should be. However, not all such hymns tread successfully the line between, on the one hand, a fully Christian presentation of God's creating, redeeming and perfecting, and on the other an overly sentimental description of 'nature' which comes perilously close to finding God to be in his creation pantheistically rather than the Lord of creation sovereignly.

Speaking of God being the sovereign Lord of creation reminds us of our first principle when considering the natural order from a Christian perspective – which is that creation cannot be fully understood unless our viewpoint is from the transcendent (i.e. God's perspective) rather than the immanent (within creation).

In recent times theories about how the universe began have become part of popular discourse as the disciplines of astronomy and physics have revealed to us remarkably precise estimations of what occurred at the beginning of things and in the first few seconds following their beginnings. That has led, in turn, to an interest in what might be called the interface between scientific and theological knowledge. Science tells us more and more about what probably happened 'at the beginning' but it can tell us nothing about what caused such a beginning because such a cause must be outside of or other than the material realm which is science's proper sphere of operation.

As the church's first thinkers engaged with the immense implications of their experience and understanding of Jesus, and his resurrection in particular, and what it all meant for an authentic appraisal of creation, they found themselves formulating a radically new way of understanding creation's status. The thought world of which they were a part accepted Greek presuppositions about the status of the world, what we call the material order. The Greek gods were not omnipotent, there being plenty of things they could not do. In particular they could not influence or change the course of Fate, that reality which apparently underpinned the varying experiences and destinies of all people. The abstract ideas concerning the material order as proposed by Greek philosophers were equally impotent when it came to offering accounts of things as genuine alternatives to the gods of mythology. The one thing that did seem to be accepted by these venerable but competing ideas was that the universe was in some sense eternal. It had always been in existence and therefore never had, and never needed, a beginning.

Against this deeply held and long-established orthodoxy the formulations of the first Christian thinkers stood out as radically new. Their proposal that the universe had been brought into being by the personal God *out of nothing* was an idea that was inconceivable in the intellectual context of the time. Irenaeus, in the latter part of the second century AD presented the logic of the Christian understanding of God's agency in creation and the implications that had for our understanding of human action and 'creating':

'While men, indeed, cannot make anything out of nothing, but only out of matter already existing, yet God is, in this point, pre-eminently superior to men, that He Himself called into being the substance of his creation, when previously it had no existence.' *(Irenaeus, 'Against Heresies', Book 2, Ch 10)*

A simple, but reasonably effective analogy for the distinction that Irenaeus is making between what it is acceptable to say about human 'creating' as opposed to God's creating is that of the potter and the clay. When humans create (i.e. make something) they do so out of material that already exists (e.g. clay). That material is then refashioned such that its resultant form can be described with a new term (i.e. pot). God's creating is such that clay itself as well as the pot is brought into being.

An important corollary of this Christian teaching about creation having been brought into being by God 'out of nothing' is that it establishes the fact that we and the rest of creation did not come out of (like an emergence from) God himself, as some alternative creation myths claim, in which they suggest that we are, in some sense, appendages to, or offspring of, God. God's bringing into being all that is 'out of nothing' means that all that is not God (i.e. creation) is distinct from God, having its own being according to God's will and purpose, with all the attendant implications that has for creation's, and especially humankind's, freedom and contingency.

This is an immensely important idea in the context of popular atheistic claims regarding religion's 'oppressive' character in which people are, apparently, deprived of their innate freedoms by religious dogma applied to the faithful like handcuffs and tightly knotted blindfolds. Of course, it is perfectly possible for religion, and indeed political ideologies, just like any human activity, to be used to deny people their dignity and freedom, and history as well as current affairs give us plenty of examples. But at the heart of a Christian understanding of our createdness in freedom (because we are distinct from God) is this wonderfully affirmative conviction about the real nature of our life as human beings. We are gifted such freedom according to God's will as an out-working of his love because the answer to the question about why God chose to create is simply that. He creates as the expression of his love. And love always desires the fullness of authentic freedom for those who are its object even in our human experience. How much more so for God. It is in this sense then that we can say that creation is a window onto God's nature (as 'love') rather than saying that because nature is so beautiful calling it God must be the best way of giving it the honour that it should rightly have.

As a way into this examination of what creation out of nothing in fact means we noted that the idea arose not from detached philosophical argumentation as a result of several possibilities being considered from which the most reasonable was chosen, but out of a deep consideration of what God's revelation of himself in Jesus Christ, and especially the risen Christ, in fact must mean.

God's work in creation is made known in the context of all that God does and intends through his living engagement, in history, with what he has brought into being. The Bible is not interested in philosophical conundrums or intellectually intriguing suggestions. It is concerned rather with the story of God's actual dealings with his creation through the history of a particular people whose own story reached its revelatory climax in the birth, ministry, death, resurrection and ascension of Jesus of Nazareth. Prayerful meditation upon the meaning of that history, through the enlightening presence of the Holy Spirit, resulted in a conception of God's work not only as being directed towards the rescue and healing of his chosen people, but also the perfecting of all creation by the mediating work of God's own Son, who, because of his incarnation, his sharing of creation's createdness, brings about the transformation of our broken world.

In other words, God's dealings with creation are personal, immersive, and oriented towards its perfecting. It is especially important to note that they are personal. They unfold in God's covenanted relationship with a particular people (Israel) and their history, and reach their climax as God himself, in the person of his Son, enters into that history in order to transform creation *from the inside*. Irenaeus brings out the distinctive character of God's entering into his creation in order to redeem it:

> [God's] only-begotten Word, who is always present with the human race, united to and <u>mingled with</u> His own creation, according to the Father's pleasure, and who became flesh, is himself Jesus Christ our Lord...' (Irenaeus, 'Against the heresies, 3.16.6) (my underlining)

As Irenaeus's expression 'mingled with' strongly suggests God does not just 'become human' in a generalized sense, as if he just turned up one day as a typical human. He becomes <u>this</u> human; the one who was born of Mary, becoming a member of a particular people as part of their unfolding story. That is part of the point of those long genealogical lists at the start of the gospels of Matthew and Luke. And in being part of that community, with its history, its shape, its character and its destiny we gain an insight into the way in which modern notions of personhood go astray. Contemporary ideas of personhood focus on its being essentially a series of decisions, choices, and actions, undertaken individualistically, unconnected with any matrix of belonging in which the person is in fact embedded. This dislocation from our historical/social

Orig. sin argument.
Consider orig. grace...

setting has particular implications for our attempts at virtue. The modern insistence on virtue as the hallmark of authentic human living rests on the performance of actions carried out by individual persons in acts of self-generated moral purity, involving, sometimes, merely the typing of a couple of angry sentences into a social media platform while sitting all alone. But what we do is as much to do with our up-bringing, our genetic predispositions, and the expectations of the societies we are part of as it is of the good (or bad) choices that we happen to make as the individual person we are. The contemporary fixation with virtuous living in societies shaped by Western culture becomes a nightmare of recrimination and accusation because it has no place for the reality of historical belonging, historical particularity, historical development, and the messiness of our fallen (sinful) nature. This is why a merely secular approach to improving behaviour can never be fully successful because it treats each person as the author of their own becoming, without reference to the deeper reality of their estrangement from their Creator, and therefore from their fellow human beings, and their participation in the cycle of moral failure which defines unregenerate human life *(Romans 7)*. Left to themselves, apparently virtuous human beings cancel each other as they weaponize guilt. God is also in the cancellation business, but only as he cancels our sin, in order that human beings can be released from the bondage of guilt through God's gifted forgiveness. We will develop these ideas in greater depth in Chapter 4 ('Person').

In an atmosphere today when humankind has become the great transgressor, the cause of so much waste, despoilment and destruction, the temptation is to heighten our perception of the non-human creation as victim. In the queue for the lifeboats the non-human part of creation is at the head of the line, in its apparent status as the primary object of God's rescue, because it deserves to be so. The hierarchy that then becomes the orthodoxy is that the non-human now supersedes the human, so that humanity's relationship with the non-human becomes that of guilty supplicant, unworthy guest, anxious onlooker. The Christian gospel then becomes, essentially, an ecological project with the environment as the beneficiary of God's grace, with humanity being relegated or even ignored, having disqualified itself by its callous exploitation of the natural world.

But the biblical pattern of humanity's relationship with the non-human creation is that humankind is itself part of the natural order and relates to the rest of the natural order as custodian, with responsibility for its flourishing. Adam and Eve are placed in the garden and given the role of gardeners, bearing in their own being the image of their creator *(Gen 1:26 – 31)*. That image is present in *them* and not in the fish, birds and reptiles etc. The hierarchy, if there is one, is of the man and woman being set 'over' the non-human with the non-human dependent to some extent on the faithful, diligent and benign management exercised by the man and woman as representatives of all humanity. To put it more bluntly, and a bit crassly, the Second Person of the Trinity becomes a man, not a banana. The New Testament delineation of this idea of the central role of humanity in creation's perfecting (filling out Genesis 1, so to speak) is the famous passage in Romans 8:

For the creation waits with eager longing for the revealing of the children of God; for the creation was subjected to futility, not of its own will but by the will of the one who subjected it, in hope that the creation itself will be set free from its bondage to decay and will obtain the freedom of the glory of the children of God. We know that the whole creation has been groaning in labour pains until now; and not only the creation, but we ourselves, who have the first fruits of the Spirit, groan inwardly while we wait for adoption, the redemption of our bodies. *(Romans 8: 19 – 23)*

It is perfectly clear from this that the perfecting of creation depends on the completion of God's work in and for humanity, in the realization of its destiny to be 'the children of God'. Consequent upon that will be creation's release from the futility it endures, a futility in which humankind is deeply implicated, of course.

Having mentioned humanity's implication in the infection of creation by a 'deathwards' dynamic (i.e. what has traditionally been called the doctrine of original sin, and its overflowing into the whole created order) it will be useful to look briefly at the Christian account of how things have gone wrong, and in particular how this relates to our understanding of creation and its destiny.

Every human community, every family and every individual knows the reality of life being in a disordered state which leads, seemingly inevitably, to disappointment, fragmentation, destruction, and death. Our own histories are littered with the results of our participation in this 'orientation to destruction' that seems to define what it means to be human.

Dismissive characterizations of the Adam and Eve story as being 'pre-scientific', or indicative of primitive naivety, miss the point. The power of the story rests in the identification of disobedience as the heart of the problem. This is perhaps why the story is so often ridiculed in contemporary Western culture because it contradicts the idea that we are masters of our own destiny. We are dismissive of a lifestyle specification that we did not concoct for ourselves. Therefore, Adam and Eve do not represent confident, self-determining, modern people. In fact they are traitors to that ideal. Their story, in modern estimation, is 'not addressed to our condition'. But, in fact, that is exactly what it is addressed to.

Pointing out contemporary rejection of the moral of the Adam and Eve story is not to suggest that modern society has no use for the concept of guilt. In fact, popular discourse accepts humanity's guilt regarding its detrimental relationship with the natural environment. Indeed, it sometimes gives the impression that punishment is the first desired outcome of activism, rather than healing (Extinction Rebellion, Just Stop Oil etc). What it does not accept is the deeper reality that selfish human behaviour points to, which is that our disordered lives are as they are, and the natural world's predicament is as it is, because of our self-elected estrangement from our Creator whose gracious 'framework for living' we have rejected. The relationship between freedom and obedience in popular culture is portrayed as one of antagonism and incompatibility. In the biblical worldview freedom is a *product* of obedience, not its antithesis. This is especially apparent when we remember that in popular culture the term 'freedom' when applied to human aspiration, almost always means 'freedom from' (e.g. freedom from constraint, obligation etc). The biblical understanding of the term freedom when applied to human being is 'freedom for' (i.e. freedom to contribute to the flourishing of the other, and consequently, or incidentally also, the self, through the enabling of the Holy Spirit).

Our petulant rejection of the truths about ourselves as set forth in this story may also point to an even deeper diagnosis of the human condition, which is that, because of our estrangement from our creator, we misconstrue our very createdness, our being as creatures, as being somehow dishonouring or belittling. We don't want to be dependent on anything or anyone, not even, and perhaps especially not even, the One from whom our very existence comes, and on whom our fulfillment depends.

The story of Adam and Eve in Genesis concentrates, quite naturally and obviously, on the reality of disordered-ness that follows their disobedience. The Garden of Eden is not pictured in any great detail. Its paradisal nature is suggested rather than described. The harmony and beauty of its original state is implied by extension from the diminishment and disfigurement that follows from the disobedience *(Gen 3: 13, 17 and 18)*. Harmony is certainly an important part of a justified description of creation in its pre-fallen state just as 'disharmony' and 'disordered-ness' capture the essence of its actual fallen state. Harmony, as a term, arises from our experience of music – the pleasing effect of different notes in combination. Perhaps this is why it seems to make perfect sense to imagine creation in its newness giving expression to its rejoicing at being 'self-consciously' alive, celebrating its 'being in freedom', through a kind of choral rejoicing – an outpouring of praise to its Creator in which each element of creation contributes its own note to the multi-layered harmony of the whole. When C S Lewis described the rising crescendo of God's creating 'in the beginning' in 'The Magician's Nephew' (*The Chronicles of Narnia*) he chose singing as the best way of characterizing both the process of creation's emergence, and the response of the different elements of creation to their being created:

'A chorus of new voices then joined the First Voice and, at the same instant, a multitude of stars, constellations, and planets appeared! "If you had seen and heard it...you would have felt quite certain that it was the stars themselves which were singing, and that it was the First Voice, the deep one, which had made them appear and made them sing." The song then continued to its climax: The Voice rose and rose, till all the air was shaking with it. And just as it swelled to the mightiest and most glorious sound it had yet produced, the sun arose." *(C S Lewis, 'The Magician's Nephew', p 61- 62)*

As we noticed in our consideration of 'Time' it seems that there is something about music and its relationship with meaning that sits deeper than mere analogy. Harmony is the ideal that humanity finds hardest to achieve because it is the pleasing outcome of particularities coming into positive inter-relationship with other particularities. Difference becomes not a problem to be removed by enforced homogeneity, nor a difficulty to be grudgingly endured, but a gift that opens up previously unimagined possibilities and satisfactions. We are imagining harmony as the soundtrack of creation 'in the beginning'. Perhaps this is best justified by the Bible's employment of exactly this soundtrack in its description of the consummation of creation in the Book of Revelation, in which the elders and saints are depicted as singing God's praises, and singing their account of what God has done and is doing *(Rev 5: 9 – 10, 7: 12, 14: 3)*. This is not to suggest that the biblical concept of consummation and perfecting, the bringing of creation to its good and ordained end, as poetically described in the Book of Revelation, is in effect a return to its original, pre-fall, state, on account of musical harmony illuminating the end as well as, in our imagination, the beginning. A number of early Christian teachers (e.g. Origen) entertained this idea of the trajectory of creation being that of 'return'. That idea cannot be mined from the biblical quarry. The biblical picture is not 'return,' but transformation into that which is gloriously re-made and fulfilled, as must be the case if we take the bodily resurrection of Jesus Christ as the measure by which creation's destiny is to be understood.

The Adam and Eve story says much about how things have been, and why they are as they are now because of its penetrating exposition of the reality and true dynamics of sin. In other words, sin is seen as something which colours and even determines both the past and the present. Countless divorcees would testify to this truth, regardless of the complex series of actions and inactions that lay behind any particular divorce. But the Christian account of sin, although it is for obvious reasons based on events in the past, is also 'forward facing'. That is to say, it declares that the whole truth about humanity and its setting (creation itself) cannot be properly understood unless it is seen from the end as well as the beginning. That is part of the logic of creation 'from nothing' – that having an actual beginning it must also therefore have an end. And because of God's covenant faithfulness that end cannot be taken to be simply extinction, due to a cosmic holocaust or a cosmic entropy, but must be the full outworking of the triumph over death that the resurrection of Jesus Christ has inaugurated. In conquering death through the resurrection of Jesus Christ God has conquered sin because sin is what causes death *(Genesis 3:19, Romans 5:12).* Therefore, creation is indeed not merely 'event' (in the past), nor a mysterious, beautiful but sullied present reality, but also something that is moving towards a future perfecting, in which:

'[God] will wipe away every tear from their eyes. There will be no more death or mourning or crying or pain for the old order of things has passed away.' *(Rev 21:4)*

God's project, which is what creation could be called, will be propelled towards, by the work of the Holy Spirit, what God has ordained that it should become.

Looking as honestly as possible at humanity's relationship with the non-human part of creation has led us, inevitably and quite properly, into some consideration of the story of creation 'in the beginning', and of the paradigmatic role of the man and the woman in the story of the Fall. At the same time we have glanced occasionally at the shape of the biblical narrative as it stretches from the beginning to the end (Genesis to Revelation), and how that narrative hangs on the act of recreation that is the resurrection of Jesus Christ, who is God present, as a creature, in his creation, for creation's sake.

If we wanted to choose a human activity that represents an ideal of humanity's relationship with the natural world at large we would probably choose gardening, because of the way that it serves to enhance and celebrate the beauty of creation through sympathetic arrangement, conservation, and even reordering. Good gardeners allow the natural order to do its thing in ways that it cannot so easily do when left simply to itself. The Garden of Eden is probably the most famous garden in human history (even though it cannot be visited either recreationally or archaeologically). The fact that the biblical Eden is not the only example of horticultural representations of paradise in world literature is no great surprise given the universal yearning for an idealized realm of beauty and delight (e.g. Persian mythology, in which the terms 'paradise' and 'garden' are more or less synonymous).

Christian meditation on the theme of gardens in the context of salvation history has provided us with some captivating and fruitful imagery. G K Chesterton exploited the possibilities in this way as part of his meditation on the implications of Jesus' resurrection:

'On the third day the friends of Christ coming at day-break to the place found the grave empty and the stone rolled away. In varying ways they realised the new wonder; but even they hardly realised that the world had died in the night. What they were looking at was the first day of a new creation, with a new heaven and a new earth; and in the semblance of the gardener God walked again in the garden, in the cool not of the evening, but the dawn.' *(G K Chesterton, 'The Everlasting Man', p 247)*

In fact when it comes to the place of gardens in the biblical story of creation's beginning, and then its ultimate perfecting, the Garden of Eden and the Resurrection Garden (if the setting of John 20: 11 – 18 may be so described) do indeed give us important insights into creation's true condition. But there is another equally important biblical garden, without which our understanding of creation's true status will remain incomplete, and that is the Garden of Gethsemane.

It is in the Garden of Gethsemane that the drama of creation's despoiling and renewing approaches its resolution. We will delve much more deeply into the important dimensions of meaning regarding Jesus that are revealed in what happened at Gethsemane in chapter 4 ('Person'), especially as it directs our thinking about what it means to be a person, as opposed to simply a human being. But, for now, we are merely noting that, as Jesus recoils in horror at the fate that awaits him, we see not a divine being acting out a role, nor an insulated approximation of a man giving a performance of deep anguish, but a real man, exposed in isolation (his closest friends are dozing some distance away), shuddering in the path of approaching Death. The detail of the account is revealing. In his extreme terror and anguish his sweat 'falls like drops of blood to the ground' *(Luke 22:44)*. Although very rare, this phenomenon is recognized medically (hematohidrosis). It affects victims in a state of extreme distress, especially when faced with physical danger (as before a battle). It is as if by describing the impact of this confrontation with evil in physical and bodily terms, the gospel account forces us, its readers, to acknowledge that the healing of creation, in which Gethsemane acts as a kind of prelude, must be carried out *materially*.

It is at this point in our reflection that it is useful to recall how St Paul, in discussing God's wonderful transformation of creation through the resurrection of Jesus Christ, uses Eden and Adam as his reference point. The healing of the disease that Adam's disobedience unleashed is achieved by the 'last (second) Adam' who is Jesus *(1 Corinthians 15:45)*. In the circumstances created by Adam's disobedience, creation's disorder and its bondage to decay and death, the undoing of that disorder and the restoration of creation's harmony and delight should be the responsibility of the one whose actions have triggered the disorder. Having failed in his appointment as custodian, protecter and benevolent director of creation, justice demands that he now relates to creation as its redeemer, its saviour, its re-creator. It is up to him to repair the damage that has been done.

It doesn't take more than a second or two to acknowledge that whether we call it humanity's 'fallen' state, or whether we use a more neutral adjective like 'flawed' or 'disturbed', humanity has not only failed to repair the damage it has caused but is incapable, without the grace of God, of doing so. What the first Adam could not do the second Adam *has* done – and he has done it as 'Adam' in the sense that he is a man. Justice's demand that a *man* put things right has been served completely and triumphantly through the second Adam, by the enabling of the Spirit, to the glory of the Father.

The honest realism of the Christian account of humanity's self-inflicted brokenness, and by extension creation's damaged state, is the necessary starting point for any truthful account of our complex relationship with nature, shot through as it is with the scars of exploitation, notwithstanding the continuing ability of nature itself to surprise us with its resilience and its capacity for self-disclosure in response to respectful scientific enquiry. Left to itself humanity can never single-handedly bring about the re-creation that creation longs for. The Christian good news is that, in fact, humanity has not been left to itself. As John Henry Newman put it in his well-known hymn 'Praise to the Holiest in the Height':

'O loving wisdom of our God!

When all was sin and shame

A second Adam to the fight

And to the rescue came. *(J H Newman, 1868)*

We described humanity as being incapable of repairing the damage it has caused 'without the grace of God'. That is a vital qualifier because it reminds us that despair is not an option for a Christianly shaped response to the ecological crisis – neither despair at humanity's repeat offending, nor despair regarding creation's ultimate destiny. Having made reference to 'the grace of God' it is important that we do not allow our thinking about this important dynamic to be watered down by the sometimes trivial or misguided uses of the phrase that we encounter in common discourse. It tends, either, to be a faintly superstitious comment on the unpredictable nature of ordinary life – 'there, but for the grace of God….', or in more overtly religious contexts, grace is thought of as being some kind of substance, like a performance enhancing additive to the fuel you need for getting through the day or the task ahead. The church in its official capacity and practice has often used this model. The biblical, and therefore fully Christian, meaning of the term is simply 'the living and active presence of the risen Lord with His attentive and obedient followers, in the Spirit, for their benefit' *(2 Cor 12:19, 2 Cor 13:13, Gal 5:4, Eph 2:5, 1Tim 1:14, 2 Tim 2:1)*

This gives us a perspective on the Christian community (the church) that allows us to see it as the place where hope shapes living, and therefore the place where the life that is lived 'in the Spirit' expresses the optimism of the gospel – that embracing of life which is utterly realistic (because it knows what, in Christ, has been overcome) and utterly joyful (because it knows that the power of the resurrection is at loose in the world). We saw how Eden and Gethsemane force us to abandon all thoughts of creation being saved through some kind of disembodied, spiritualized, metaphysical transaction, because of the bodily materiality of the one through whom salvation must be achieved, a bodily reality made painfully explicit on the cross. The resurrection of Christ, if it is to have any kind of integrity with the emphatic materiality of all that precedes it, must be the triumphant manifestation of his transformed body, and not merely a narrative expression of a 'spiritual experience', as it has sometimes been interpreted.

That being the case, we can start to see how this intense pinpointing of God's involvement with his creation in the life, death, and resurrection of his Son in that place, at that time, raises our understanding of creation's status to a level that is unmatched by any competing philosophy or world view. Christianity is, from this perspective, utterly materialistic because it accords to the material order a meaning and destiny that affirms it in its materiality ('and God saw that it was *good*.' Gen 1), while also seeing it as caught up into an eternal destiny by the incarnation, resurrection, and ascension of Jesus Christ, the Son of God. In the Christian world, matter does indeed matter. We can wholeheartedly affirm creation's materiality not because creation is self-sufficiently material as if it stood alone in the universe, but because its Creator has endowed it with eternal meaning and purpose. That meaning and purpose will in due time be revealed when the New Jerusalem appears:

'Then I saw a new heaven and a new earth; for the first heaven and the first earth had passed away, and the sea was no more. And I saw the holy city, the new Jerusalem, coming down out of heaven from God, prepared as a bride adorned for her husband.' *(Rev 21: 1 – 2)*

As we have looked at the role of the Spirit in making Jesus' lived Sonship possible without denying his full humanity, we have found ourselves necessarily swimming in Trinitarian waters. Looking at any Christian doctrine always takes us eventually into an engagement with God's revelation of Himself as Father, Son and Holy Spirit, and this is especially so with the doctrine of creation. Indeed, it was because of that process of deep reflection on the meaning and status of Jesus Christ that followed his resurrection and ascension, as the first Christians sought to make sense of all that had happened in and through him, that the beginnings of an understanding of God as Trinity got underway. It took the church a further 300 years to get to the point where it felt able to attempt a written summary of the idea (the Councils of Nicaea, 325 AD and Constantinople, 381 AD). But as early as the second century a Christian thinker had emerged whose insights into the mystery of God's dealings with his creation were to prove decisive in the battle of ideas that shook the ancient world as Christianity's claims became more widely known. He also contributed creatively to the early church's attempts to construct analogies designed to give some conceptual shape to the extraordinary ideas about God and his relationship with creation that Christianity proposed. St Irenaeus was Bishop of

Lyon in the second half of the second century AD. The frontispiece at the beginning of this book is an icon written by a Russian friend of mine, based on the earliest extant representations of what he may have looked like. Although the intellectual battles that he fought took place over 1800 years ago their features have a remarkably contemporary feel. We will develop our meditation on some aspects of 'Nature' from a Christian perspective by taking a brief look at what Irenaeus had to say.

The main philosophical and religious competition to Christianity in Irenaeus's time was a collection of ideas about how human beings might achieve salvation through the acquisition of esoteric knowledge. The umbrella term for these philosophies is Gnosticism, from the Greek 'gnosis' meaning 'knowledge'.

Gnosticism did look attractive to the thinking person, especially one who was drawn to Christianity, because it purported to be a development of, or improvement on, Christianity. It spoke of the divine Logos, the Word of God, in the world, but only as a kind of semi-divine intermediary between the temporal and the eternal. The earthiness and simplicity of the divine Logos being a man who ate, slept and sweated – Jesus of Nazareth – was portrayed as primitive, and as an idea in need of sophisticating, especially in the context of Greek ideas about the inferiority of matter and the superiority of the spiritual and eternal realm of the mind and of the heavens.

Once you decide to take a simple idea – God amongst us as a particular man, our saviour, and elaborate it with complicated and exotic mythical layers to be mastered by contemplation and intellectual athleticism there is likely to be no end to the growing mental edifice. Gnosticism became more and more complicated and impenetrable, yet also attractive because of its apparent cleverness and its daunting challenge – in the same way that Everest is attractive to the amateur climber.

Although Gnosticism sounds exotic, and in its detail it was very exotic, it is actually not a million miles from ideas that are still widespread today. We also place 'knowledge' on a higher plane than the merely physical. Manual labour is not rewarded financially or in terms of status in the way that intellectual performance is. The divide between the apparently lower world of matter and the apparently higher world of the spirit is still deeply rooted in our thinking. The idea of the soul being 'imprisoned' in the body which decays still distorts Christian thinking. Behind it all lurks the notion that it is beneath God to be present in, or in any detailed way concerned about, the material nitty-gritty of his creation.

In other words, the Gnostics had a false doctrine of creation, and its falsity, its inadequacy, is exposed by the Incarnation.

This honouring of the world of created matter in Christianity has a very apposite and beautiful demonstration in the example of the icon. There were some people, and there still are, who thought that the making of images of the Son of God and of the saints was idolatry – and that belief was taken up and made an absolute in Islam, of course. But the Eastern church in particular has always claimed that if Christ became flesh, does that not imply a capacity for matter to represent

God? As John of Damascus put it in the great iconoclastic controversy of the eighth century:

'...when God is seen in the flesh conversing with men, I make an image of the God whom I see. I do not worship matter; I worship the Creator of matter who became matter for my sake, who wills to take His abode in matter; who worked out my salvation through matter.' (John of Damascus, 'First Apology against those who decry the Divine Images' #16, early 8*th* century)

Iconography therefore offers an important connection to the Christian doctrine of creation because it reminds us that God can speak to us through an inspired re-working of the material of this world – paint, wood, horsehair and all the rest of it. And we should also note that at the heart of Christian worship and community is the totally unambiguous demonstration that the material world can indeed represent God – in the eucharist – the materiality of bread and wine.

Irenaeus's contribution to the argument about the world and its status and destiny rested not only on his championing of the Incarnation as God's 'Yes' to his creation, but also on the brilliance of his portrayal of the role of the Holy Spirit in his work of perfecting. Rather than speaking of what might be called the 'division of labour' within the persons of the Trinity as being the Father who creates, the Son who redeems and the Spirit who sustains, he preferred 'the Father who creates, the Son who redeems, and the Spirit who perfects.'

That contribution to an understanding of the Spirit lifts the conception from the implicitly static feel of 'sustain' to the much more dynamic feel of 'perfect' because of the way in which perfecting entails movement, development and transformation. It reinforces the biblical idea of creation being God's 'project' as opposed to a finished and singular event. All these ways of characterising the Spirit's role do much better justice to him being the living God (and not just the God who stands guard or merely maintains things in being).

The difficulty of finding appropriate ways of describing God in his own being as triune, three persons in one God, is well illustrated by the length of time it took the church to arrive at an agreed formula, as we noted above. Just as difficult it seems is the likelihood of finding an analogy for the reality of the triune life of God that does at least some justice to the impossible task of imaging the un-imageable.

One of the most well-known attempts at an analogy for the Trinity is St Augustine's 'the Lover, the Loved, and the Love that passes between them' – not very good, because it swerves very obviously in the direction of 'Bi-nitarianism', reducing the Holy Spirit to a kind of shuttling avenue of relationship rather than a person in his own right. Then there are the children's talk/Sunday School over simplifications – my mother was mother, wife and daughter all at the same time etc. This tends towards Unitarianism because she is still only one person, unlike God.

Irenaeus' response to this analogy challenge was to describe the Son and the Spirit as 'the two hands of God'.

This has several big advantages over later attempts. Firstly, It allows for plurality within unity in a living or active image. We can recognise the conditional independence of each of our hands, while also recognising that they are, in the end, part of the unity which makes us a single agent of activity.

And secondly, it is a beautifully simple solution to the problem of mediation. The theological 'problem of mediation' is this. If there is a God who creates, what is his relationship with that which has been created? How is his involvement with creation mediated? Is he like a helicopter mother who can't leave her child to get on with anything by themselves? Is he so present to it, so near to it, that he is to all intents and purposes the same as it? That's pantheism, as we have seen. All theologies which emphasise his proximity run this risk.

On the other hand, is he so 'other' so different, so transcendent, that His remoteness as God equates to sheer absence – un-contactability? That's the Islamic idea – God's otherness is absolute.

Irenaeus's 'two hands' solves this problem simply and elegantly. God relates to his creation, to that which is not himself, by means of the Son and the Spirit, his 'two hands'. Creation's freedom to be itself is not violated by God's presence within it such that God's perfection overwhelms creation's imperfection simply by his being present, because by being a *man* the second person of the Trinity participates in creation's freedom and contingency. Indeed, it is God himself who is violated, on the cross. But creation is also not left ultimately to itself so that it can destroy itself. Its destiny is assured because of the work of the perfecting Spirit. Perhaps Irenaeus' analogy of the two hands encourages us to imagine God somewhat differently from the popular artistic portrayal of an old, bearded man enthroned on clouds, surrounded by

Rubenesque cherubs, looking benignly downwards. A better image might be of the 'artisan' God – sleeves rolled up in the workshop of his re-creating so that his hands can get on with the job.

Let us conclude our attempt to set out a more comprehensive account of how Christianity understands creation than simply as a 'realm of environmental crisis' by returning to the metaphor of gardens and what can be found in them.

In 1 Peter 2 we find the following reference to Christ – that he is the one 'who in his own self bore our sins in his own body on the tree.' *(1 Pet 2: 24)* Calling the cross 'a tree' in this way has afforded poets a rich vein of imagery with which to explore the connections that might be found within the sweep of salvation history.

John Donne took up the popular imaginative fancy of his time that the tree of Calvary stood in exactly the same place that the Tree of the Knowledge of good and evil had done whose fruit Adam and Eve ate – in order to bring out the deep theological connections between the two 'trees'.

He wrote a poem while on his sick-bed. It contains the following stanza:

We think that Paradise and Calvary,

Christ's cross and Adam's tree stood in one place;

Look, Lord, and find both Adams in me;

As the first Adam's sweat surrounds my face,

May the last Adam's blood my soul embrace. *(John Donne, 'Hymn to God, my God, in My Sickness', 1631)*

Adam was condemned, because of his disobedience, to sweaty toil until his death ('by the sweat of your face you shall eat bread until you return to the ground....'*Gen 3:19*). Donne does not mention it explicitly in his poem but uppermost in his mind would have been that moment in Gethsemane (on which we reflected above) when in anguish of dread the 'second Adam' contemplates his own death as his 'sweat was, as it were, great drops of blood falling to the ground.' The sweat of sickness and mortality soaks the poet's face – but the redeeming blood of the Saviour soaks his soul. And on the way from the image of sweat as a sign of death in Adam, to blood as an image of life in Christ, is Christ's blood-like sweat, or sweat-like blood.

At the start of this chapter we made reference to a lady participant in a TV show waxing lyrical about the tree in her back garden, telling us how wise it was, and how much more it knew than we mere mortals. I adopted a tone of amused ridicule in my account. But actually, Brain-tree lady, as I called her, was on the one hand in very good company, and on the other, closer to the truth than she realised. The good company she was keeping was with none other than Eve herself, as portrayed by Milton in Paradise Lost. After Eve had taken the fruit Milton has her saying to the tree:

'O Sovereign, virtuous, precious of all Trees in Paradise' – and she goes on to tell the tree that she will tend it each morning with daily praise, and she genuflects before it. We could be forgiven for thinking that that Braintree back garden was actually the site of Eden. Eve and Braintree lady are clearly soul-mates.

That's the 'good company' dimension of Brain-tree lady. The 'closer to the truth' dimension is that she reminds us, although she would not put it this way, that we have a choice of worshipping tree, or tree. We can go down on one knee before the tree of nature, or the tree of life – that tree which, although it was the tree of death for the man who hung on it, was in fact the tree of life for us.

George Herbert, who rivals Donne for the reputation of being the greatest of the English Metaphysical poets, as they are sometimes called, was also drawn to the possibilities of comparing the tree of Eden with the tree of Calvary. In his lengthy poem 'Sacrifice' the speaker is Christ, addressing from the cross, those who gaze on him. One stanza goes like this:

'O all ye who pass by, behold and see

Man stole the fruit but I must climb the tree,

The tree of Life to all but only Me:

Was ever grief like mine?'

Herbert titled his poem 'Sacrifice', and we are familiar with the notion of Christ's death on the cross being interpreted as a sacrifice which cancels sin. As the Letter to the Hebrews reminds us it is because of who is being sacrificed that the old system of sacrifice as a technique designed to allow sinful human beings access to God and his forgiveness was now redundant. Jesus' life and death are now the way into God's presence – as symbolised by the tearing of the temple veil in two, thereby opening the Holy of Holies to all.

But Jesus' death on the cross does not exhaust the possibilities of 'sacrifice' as the idea might relate to a follower of Christ. Irenaeus, who we met a little earlier, re-cast the idea of sacrifice by interpreting its true meaning for the followers of Christ in the light of Christ's death as 'a human being truly alive.' He meant that for those who accept Christ's life and death as being for them, and who therefore know the indwelling power of the Holy Spirit, these are they who are in fact a 'living sacrifice, holy and pleasing to God' and by dint of this are now 'truly alive'. This is sacrifice as a thanksgiving offering that we make to God, after the pattern of Jesus own self-offering to his Father.

As we contemplate the sacrifices that may have to be made as part of our renewed stewardship of creation we could do worse than keep in mind Irenaeus' arresting definition of the beneficiaries of Jesus' life and death as they share his sacrifice. By God's grace our prospects are not limited to becoming self-condemned victims of the planet's demise but truly alive agents of God's healing hands, his Son and Spirit.

Language

One of our light-hearted analogies when looking at the fascinating relationship between time and music in chapter 1 concerned the comedy sketch involving Morecambe and Wise and their guest celebrity Andre Previn. Eric Morecambe's punchline, following the fiasco of his redefinition of the piano entry in Grieg's 1st Piano Concerto was 'I'm playing all the right notes. But not necessarily in the right order.'

Samuel Taylor Coleridge (1772 – 1834), the critic, theologian, and poet, might not thank me for putting him in company with Morecambe and Wise, but it is difficult not to be reminded by Eric Morecambe's punchline of Samuel Taylor Coleridge's definition of a poem as being 'the best words in the best order.' (*Henry Nelson Coleridge*, *'Specimens of Table Talk by Samuel Taylor Coleridge'*, *1835*)

A human being reflecting on the significance of language is a bit like a fish reflecting on the significance of water. Life as we experience it is, quite literally, unimaginable, impossible to conceive, without language, because thought itself can only be undertaken by using language as its medium, to say nothing of the commerce of ideas, descriptions, and person to person interaction that written and spoken language makes possible. This being the case it is important that the scope of this reflection is carefully defined. 'Language' as such is too vast a field to do justice to in a mere chapter of a modest book. Interesting though it might be to delve into questions about how language came into being, and how it forms a big part of what makes us human, and similar investigations, that is not our ambition here. More precisely we are concerning ourselves with words, which are of course the building blocks of language, and with how Christian belief invites us to attend to God who has revealed himself as the God who speaks, and who is therefore known through language, can be communicated with through language (especially prayer) and who, when he comes among us, is described as 'Word.' *(John 1: 1)*

In due course we will also reflect on the implications of what is properly meant by the Christian scriptures being referred to as 'the word of God', and, returning to Samuel Taylor Coleridge's aphorism concerning poetry, we will look at the power of poetry when it is employed to open up theological truths in ways that mere prose cannot match.

Given that religions concern themselves with what are sometimes called ultimate things (i.e. deep questions about existence, purpose and destiny) it comes as no surprise to notice that they generate vast quantities of written and spoken material in their attempts to describe, argue about, elaborate upon, celebrate and proclaim what they believe. When the author of John's gospel took stock of his efforts to summarise the story of Jesus, into which he had woven the full theological implications of the remarkable story he was telling, based on a few carefully chosen highlights, he noted that were anyone to attempt an equally elaborate and allusive telling of the whole unedited story the written output would be overwhelming:

'…there are also many other things that Jesus did; if every one of them were written down I suppose that the world itself could not contain the books that would be written.' *(John 21: 25)*

A strong case could be made for the proposition that Christianity is the 'wordiest' religion of all. Its Holy Scriptures are a mixture of saga or myth, history, poetry, prophecy, biography, philosophy, apocalyptic (the 'unveiling' of matters to do with the end of the story of creation), exhortation and parable, to name just some of the main types of literature contained within it. One way or another the subject matter is God, and his dealings with what he has brought into being. Not only is the story the Bible tells rich in drama and variety, requiring, one might say, the wide range of literature that we have just listed in order to do justice to the subject matter; it is also pregnant with meaning and implication. The reader is not simply engaged in an act of familiarization. She is caught up in a process of discovery, not just of the events and ideas described, and the authors' interpretations of them, but also of herself as the Holy Spirit starts his work of sanctifying and perfecting. In a sense the scriptures read us even more than we read them.

The knowledge of God and the life he gives as mediated by the scriptures and experienced in the life of the church has, naturally and inevitably, given rise to a vast secondary literature of reflection, analysis, discussion and depiction. Academic theology is at the heart of this enterprise and alongside it are countless examples of devotional and poetic articulation adding their voices to the human attempt to say something about God. Even the words of this faltering reflection are in their own tiny way an addition to this immense library.

Yet, despite all this there is a sense in which words are insufficient, indeed presumptuous even. Many of the saints, and those who are wise, who have trod the path of discipleship in the past, have reminded us that the difference between God and what he has created is of an order, and of such magnitude, that it cannot be measured or truly described from our limited human perspective and circumstance. This is a truth that we touched on in Chapter 2 when we talked about the implications of creation being brought into being by God 'out of nothing'. Our otherness from God is his gift, and on this fact is based our freedom. But so also is God's 'unknowability', which is simply a way of saying that no words that we might press into the service of understanding and 'grasping' God can fully achieve that end. The gulf that separates an ant from a Nobel Prize winner is considerable, but that which separates the Nobel Prize winner from God is, quite literally, immeasurable.

There is an honourable tradition within Christianity, which is not unrelated to the mystical tradition, which seeks to give full value to the knowing of God that goes beyond words, in the sense of leaving words behind. It recognises that encountering God in his awe-ful majesty and burning love must leave us dumbstruck, and that being rendered incapable of speech, far from being a kind of failure, would in fact be a sign of authenticity, of utter reality. It would amount to speechless surrender into the arms of the divine Lover.

St John of the Cross is probably the best know exemplar of this branch of Christian spirituality. In trying to express the ineffable he is forced to use words, but only in order to give expression to experiences and perceptions that, paradoxically, defy verbal definition. Not surprisingly his style teeters on the edge of obscurity and contradiction. In his 'Stanzas Concerning an Ecstasy Experienced in High Contemplation' he strains the coherence of language itself in his attempt to portray a rapturous state of contemplation:

1. I entered into unknowing,
yet when I saw myself there,
without knowing where I was,
I understood great things;
I will not say what I felt
for I remained in unknowing
transcending all knowledge.

2. That perfect knowledge
was of peace and holiness
held at no remove
in profound solitude;
it was something so secret
that I was left stammering,
transcending all knowledge.

(St John of the Cross, late 16th century)

The experience of the presence of God places him in a realm of knowing that cannot be reduced to words – hence the 'stammering, transcending all knowledge.'

Being aware of the limitations of language can offer useful protection from the desire to capture God by careful and apparently accurate description. There is some overlap here with the ancient idea that naming something, defining its identity, confers power over that which is named. The line between employing words with ingenuity and imagination in order to align our definitions more closely with the truth they seek to affirm about God, and making those words a limiting of what God can be, is one that philosophers and theologians have not always successfully negotiated.

G K Chesterton took aim at our over-reliance on verbal definitions of a simplistic sort when he described that attitude as believing in 'the infallibility of language.' He put it this way:

'Every time one man says to another, 'Tell us plainly what you mean' he is assuming the infallibility of language: that is to say, he is assuming that there is a perfect scheme of verbal expression for all the internal moods and meanings of men. Whenever a man says to another, 'Prove your case; defend your faith,' he is assuming the infallibility of language: that is to say, he is assuming that a man has a word for every reality in earth, or heaven, or hell. He knows that there are in the soul tints more bewildering, more numberless, more nameless, than the colours of an autumn forest.....Yet he seriously believes that these things can every one of them, in all their tones and semi-tones, in all their blends and unions, be accurately represented by an arbitrary system of grunts and squeals.....' *(G K Chesterton, 'G K Chesterton on G F Watts', Watts Gallery, 2008)*

In other words, mystical spirituality faces up to the limitation of words because it wants to go beyond them. But even words used to articulate what we understand of God and his ways at the day-to-day level, as in sermons, or books about God, can only tell part of the story, as Chesterton colourfully asserts.

It may seem slightly odd that we have started our thinking about words and the part they play in our knowing of God by focusing on their inadequacy. We lined up on the start-line, and then, when the gun went off, we went backwards, apparently. The reason for approaching our subject in this way is simply to emphasise the dangers of slipping into a mindset which thinks that words about God are an end in themselves; that because God is transcendentally other than us the best we can hope for is to strive to give articulation to the thoughts and hopes that inspire and disturb us, and that this striving is worthy of celebration. This is the dangerous territory that theologians and philosophers inhabit, both the professionals and the amateurs. C S Lewis identified and reflected on this danger in his poem 'The Apologist's Evening Prayer':

From all my lame defeats and oh! much more
From all the victories that I seemed to score;
From cleverness shot forth on Thy behalf
At which, while angels weep, the audience laugh;
From all my proofs of Thy divinity,
Thou, who wouldst give no sign, deliver me.

Thoughts are but coins. Let me not trust, instead
of Thee, their thin-worn image of Thy head.
From all my thoughts,
even from my thoughts of Thee,
O thou fair Silence, fall, and set me free.
Lord of the narrow gate and the needle's eye,
Take from me all my trumpery lest I die.

(C S Lewis, 'The Apologist's Evening Prayer', in 'Poems', 1964)

The distinction we are seeking to grasp is captured in the opening lines of the second verse ('Thoughts are but coins. Let me not trust, instead of Thee, their thin-worn image of Thy head.') '...instead of Thee'. That's the danger. Our business is with God himself, the living God, and not with ideas and verbal formulations, nor even worthy approximations of the truth — but with Truth himself.

This brings us inexorably, and indeed happily, to the heart of the matter as far as a Christian account of words and God is concerned. To concentrate on the perilous activity of speaking about God, with all its pitfalls and problems is a valuable prelude but it cannot be the sum of what must be said. God is indeed unknowable if we are left to construct a pathway to such knowledge through our own earthbound efforts. That is part of the tragedy of the story of the Tower of Babel as recorded in Genesis 11. But we are not left to our own devices, our own ingenuity, or our own well-meaning exertions. The writer to the Hebrews tells us how things actually work when it comes to our knowledge of God. He spells it out in his opening declaration:

'Long ago God spoke to our ancestors in many and various ways by the prophets, but in these last days he has spoken to us by a Son...' *(Hebrews 1: 1 – 2)*

John Webster, speaking of this fact of God's choosing to address us, and not our choosing to address him, puts it like this; 'The agency, we should note, is God's: eschatological existence (i.e. the church living in God's resurrection time) is not a discovery, still less an invention, but a disclosure.' *(John Webster, 'God Without Measure', p66)*

That is to say, God is the God who speaks, and his speech is his action since God's words are the enacting of his will and his choice. They bring into being that which he wills. So, in Genesis 1, in the account of God's creating, God *said* 'Let there be light'. The whole account is a reporting of God's successive declarations of his will when in each case he speaks, and things come to be. The prophet Isaiah gives a poetic affirmation of this fundamental fact about God's speaking being one side of the coin whose other side is God's creating:

'For as the rain and snow come down from heaven, and do not return there until they have watered the earth, making it bring forth and sprout, giving seed to the sower and bread to the eater, so shall my word be that goes out from my mouth: it shall not return to me empty, but it shall accomplish that which I purpose, and succeed in the thing for which I sent it.' *(Isaiah 55: 10 – 11)*

It is almost impossible to overstate the significance of God being the one who takes the initiative in the 'commerce of communication' that exists between himself and humanity. This is especially important in the face of assertions which are now so commonplace in the forum of contemporary debate about where a template for good living might be found. As we saw with 'Braintree' woman, and others like her, the assumption in society at large is that personal freedom can be expressed by self-construction. Following the example of Rousseau, attending to the spiritual dimension of life amounts to the domestication or appropriation of God, so that God becomes an aspect of self-consciousness or self-construction. Explanations and descriptions of this spirituality by those who practice it draw on their own experience of life and their own search for meaning. Their spirituality tree is planted in the soil of their own life story and the nutrients it supplies are, by definition, self-generated and self-referential. Some words of Dietrich Bonhoeffer throw a penetrating light on such error:

Our salvation is 'from outside ourselves' (extra nos). I find salvation, not in my life story, but only in the story of Jesus Christ…What we call our life, our troubles, and our guilt is by no means the whole of reality; our life, our need, our guilt, and our deliverance are there in the Scriptures.' *(Dietrich Bonhoeffer, 'Life Together', p62)*

It is, then, inevitable that such self-constructed spiritualities are highly individualistic because they are each shaped by a single human life, with all its limitations. Attempts have sometimes been made to establish 'new age' style worship communities based on some kind of bedrock of common belief held by those who might be attracted to such an experiment. They never last very long because, notwithstanding some shared ideas (usually relating to pantheistic attitudes towards the natural world), the idea of a common creed and practice undermines the inherent individuality of each potential member's 'lifestyle spirituality'.

In direct contrast to this stands the Christian approach to life in the community which God creates. The vision of that redeemed and perfected community as described in the Book of Revelation is the New Jerusalem – *coming down* from heaven. It does not come into being by human decision making, so that something can be built from the ground up, based on earthly resources and the idealisms of men and women. It comes 'down' as a gift from God himself, and he invites us into membership of the New Jerusalem on the basis not of our enthusiasm, or our abilities, or our 'vision' of a better world, but on the basis of surrender. The giving up of self. The turning away from self-justification, especially our self-justifying moral posturing, and the taking up of a cross, the cross that speaks of Jesus' self-surrender as the gateway to a new creation.

The opening words of the Letter to the Hebrews, which we quoted above, set out very clearly this fundamental fact about divine/human communication – that it is, first and foremost, from God, to us: 'God spoke to our ancestors....but in these last days he has spoken to us by a Son.' This formulation, in Hebrews 1: 1 – 2, of exactly how God addresses us is of the utmost importance as we attend to the whole matter of the place of words in our knowledge of God.

It is part of our instinctive way of thinking as human beings, I suppose, that when we imagine a communication from God addressed to us his creatures, we take it to be in a form of words. There is apparent justification for this, both in the biblical tradition, where Moses brings down from God at Mt Sinai, the words of God concerning the framework of living that he gives to his people, and in other religious traditions (e.g. Islam, where according to orthodox Islamic belief, God's very utterances are recorded in the Qur'an). The biblical account of God's speaking is rooted, initially, in the tradition of the prophets declaring the word of God, the word that has come to them in order for it to be passed on to the people as they hear it relayed, so to speak, through the prophet.

Because the prophets lived at a certain time and in a certain place as part of the kaleidoscope of political, religious and social forces which formed the context for their prophecy, their words and deeds are recorded in the Old Testament in the language of that time and place; Hebrew. They bear witness to the struggle that the community had with what sort of people they should be in the light of their peculiar history, and of the calling that God had given them as it contrasted with the religious practices of other peoples. Part of the prophetic message was that Israel's calling was to fulfill a destiny ordained by God, and that destiny was not defined according to their own national aspirations, or even God's apparent intentions to favour them with the trappings of their 'chosen' status. It was, rather, to be a people in whom God's loving purposes for all people could be shown forth, and in that showing would be seen to be sacrificial in nature. They were to be God's people for others. The prophet Isaiah put it like this, speaking of Israel's status as those in whom his purpose will be fulfilled:

[God] says, 'It is too light a thing that you should be my servant to raise up the tribes of Jacob and to restore the survivors of Israel; I will give you as a light to the nations, that my salvation may reach the ends of the earth.' *(Isaiah 49:6)*

There is a deep mystery at work in the long story of Israel's struggle to come to terms with the implications of being a people for others. Alongside the intense desire to have a home, a place which could be called their own, which runs like a theme through so much of their history (Abraham's journeying, the escape from Egypt, the wandering in the desert, the Exile from that home and the return to it, and more recently the establishment of the modern state of Israel) is also the dark history of marginalization, persecution, and the threat of utter destruction. The prophet Amos expressed the troubling implications of such a calling in its stark realism. Speaking of the chosen people of Israel he announces God's declaration:

'You only have I known of all the families of the earth; therefore, I will punish you for all your iniquities.' *(Amos 3:2)*

A complaint that is sometimes made by those who are scandalized by God's apparent favouritism can be countered by reference to the challenging nature of God's calling of Israel as it is defined by Amos, and confirmed in the nation's actual history, of which the Holocaust is the appalling summation. With 'favouritism' like that who would want to be favoured? The same complaint can also take the form of a ridiculing of the specificity of God's engagement, an impatience with the particularity. If God really is interested in everyone, so runs the argument, why doesn't he simply convey his intentions and confirm his identity by a kind of mass spiritual vaccination program in which everyone gets an enlightening beam from heaven straight into their consciousness. Why all this messy, ambiguous and inconclusive stuff about a people whose religious representatives appear to be a pretty unattractive bunch of jeremiad addicted spoilsports? Why not by-pass all that and make saintliness a kind of extra chromosome that everyone is born with?

As soon as we put it like that the flaw in the proposal starts to become apparent. The chief casualty of such a programme of enforced 'God-connectedness' would be our freedom, particularly our freedom to say 'No' to God, and also, of course, our freedom to say 'Yes' to him. Rather than confining himself to the inside of our heads via the laser beam of enlightenment where no-one can see inside anyone else's head to see if what they are experiencing is exactly the same as what's going on inside their own head, he chooses not the realm of private, invisible, religious experience but the public arena of historical unfolding, the life of a particular people, which becomes a canvas open to scrutiny and interrogation by anyone interested in what God is apparently saying. The path to universal knowledge of God is, and in fact can only be, through the historically particular.

But although there is no way round the particular as the locus of God's engagement with humanity there is still the issue of words – the words that the prophets use to impart the content of God's speaking. Those words are the vehicles of God's meaning, but they are also part of the matrix of human striving. This is the big difference between the Christians' holy book and the holy books of other religions, Islam in particular. The texts of the Bible are part of the literary history of humankind, albeit a very special part. They are not a written version of the 'laser beam direct from heaven' idea. They are the words of that particular people in the context of the Spirit's judgmental and providential fashioning of them into God's people for all people. And they are words which need translating if others are to know what they mean, to say nothing of the imprecision that Chesterton was railing against in his broadside against the notion of the 'infallibility of language'.

In the face of this apparent difficulty let us recall again that opening declaration made by the author of the Letter to the Hebrews:

'Long ago God spoke to our ancestors in many and various ways by the prophets, but in these last days he has spoken to us by a Son...' *(Hebrews 1:1)*

The testimony is not that the Son delivered a spoken or written manifesto, or some fascinating parables, nor even some startling re-definitions, delivered in appropriately beautiful rhetoric, of God's nature and purpose to be eagerly recorded by his rapt followers. The testimony is that God has spoken to us *by a Son*; which is to say that the language he is using is the language of the life, death and resurrection of Jesus of Nazareth. In other words, God has moved beyond the limitations of language in the prosaic sense, and encapsulated all that he means to say in the 'language' of the person who is

Son. This is the main thrust of the use of the name for Jesus ('Word') that John uses at the start of his gospel.

'In the beginning was the Word, and the Word was with God, and the Word was God.' *(John 1:1)*

Words are the conveyors of meaning, and it seems that John is interested not simply in giving an account of the brief but extraordinary life of Jesus of Nazareth, but in alerting us to the fact that in this life all meaning pertaining to humankind – the puzzles and paradoxes of our existence, and the pains and pleasures of our comings and goings, is articulated and interpreted. In his meditations on the way in which the simple things of everyday life can be vehicles for God's address to us Harry Blamires turns his attention to the most everyday thing of all things – the thing we call 'a word' and what the Christian might learn of God through what we call a word:

'Small wonder that, though you can say 'Man is a word,' or 'Garden is a word' you cannot say 'A man is a word,' or 'A garden is a word.' But you can say 'Christ is a word,' and then say, 'Christ is the Word.' The Word, not a word. The vehicle of all meaning. The key to all meaning.' *(Blamires, 'The Marks of the Maker', p180)*

It is a truism to say that actions speak louder than words. That truism acknowledges a hierarchy of authenticity. Words do convey truth, but in human experience they can be diluted by ambiguity or negated by insincerity. The husband who tells his wife on the day before her birthday that he loves her, but then forgets the next morning to get her that lovely bunch of roses is the epitome of our fallenness. Sin is that which disintegrates our being *('Woe is me! I am lost.' Isaiah 6:5)*. The Hebrew translated here as 'lost' contains the idea of 'disintegrated' so that we become, at heart, inherently contradictory, incoherent, dis-integrated. Our actions say a different thing from our words.

But, as we have noted, there is no tension between God's words and God's action. The words of God lead not to contradiction and destruction but to coherence and creation. And what appears to us as two aspects of God's living being – his speaking, and his acting, come together in the Word who is God addressing himself to us as the One in whom and through whom creation is enacted and perfected.

Perhaps the most evocative and poetically powerful summary of the whole extraordinary story of God's speaking to us 'by a Son' is the announcement embedded in John's prelude to his gospel, what we call chapter 1:

'And the Word was made flesh, and dwelt among us, and we beheld his glory, the glory as of the only begotten of the Father, full of grace and truth.' *(John 1:14, KJV)*

As we explore the place of words in our knowledge of God we should try and say something about all those words which form the context for John's beautiful summary – the Holy Scriptures themselves. We have already alluded to the fact that the Christian scriptures are not quite the same sort of thing as the holy writings found in other religions. A good way of highlighting this important distinction is to ask the question 'Where, according to religious claims, is God to be 'seen' most unambiguously?' In some religious traditions the answer to that question is given in the form – 'in these writings', those writings being the holy writings of that particular religion. And in much of the Christian world the answer would take the same form. God is to be 'seen' most unambiguously in the 'word of God', the Holy Scriptures, the Bible.

If you do a quick survey of the content of many Religious Studies textbooks produced for use with children, even older children, you will notice a section on 'holy writings'. In one way or another, books such as the Qur'an, the Bhagavad-Gita, the Guru Granth Sahib and the Bible are grouped together as examples of a common phenomenon. It's a lazy and misleading approach. It appears to assume that, broadly speaking, we are dealing with the same sort of thing whenever we pick up an example from this apparently homogeneous category. A Muslim and a Sikh might concede that there is a very superficial commonality between the Qur'an and the Guru Granth Sahib as far as status and function are concerned, but not at the deeper level of origin or authorship.

The inappropriateness of placing the Bible in such a list becomes starkly apparent when we acknowledge that a Christian's answer to the question 'Where, according to religious claims, is God to be 'seen' most unambiguously?' is not 'the Bible', but 'Jesus Christ.'

'Whoever has seen me has seen the Father.' (John14:9) – not, we might add, 'whoever has read the scriptures has seen the Father.')

Part of the instinct to treat the Bible as an infallible and fixed manifestation of God's identity and 'history' arises from a desire for certainty. At the human or psychological level, that is very understandable. In the midst of the maelstrom of life a firm rock to which we might anchor ourselves seems essential, and treating the Bible as that rock becomes the sub-text of a certain sort of 'bible based' preaching and teaching. Added to this is the powerful undertow exerted by our culture's commitment to the superiority of knowledge provided by science, with all its attractive appearance of certainty and its apparent banishment of doubt. (We should reiterate that this is not the claim of 'science' as such, but of scientism.) To place the Bible on a plinth of granite-like certainty makes the mistake of tacitly accepting scientism's approach to truth. It leads to the absurdity of the doctrine of inerrancy – that every statement in the Bible must, by definition, be factually accurate. The conceptual contortions made necessary by this approach can be imagined when, for example, some justification is attempted which aims to preserve the inerrancy principle in the light of the contradictory accounts of Judas's death. Matthew 27:5 has Judas hanging himself, while Acts 1:18 has him falling headlong to the ground in the field he bought with the High Priests' money, with his lower torso bursting open. The Judas example could be called a glaring one, but many other apparently less glaring ones could also be cited, including the difficulties that arise when trying to reconcile Romans 13 ('obey your earthly rulers for they have been appointed by God') with Revelation 13 ('the earthly authorities, as exampled by Rome, are the enemies of God's purposes of justice and peace').

There is some (unintended) irony in the kind of approach to Holy Scripture that we have just characterized (in which it is, apparently, the inerrant 'word of God') in that, despite its claim to elevate the Bible to a supreme position of authority and status, its approach is actually an elevation of the user of the Bible, as the user imposes on it his own scheme of interpretation, which goes against the grain of the Bible's actual nature. In this respect the fundamentalist (as he is sometimes called) shares the same presuppositions as his arch-enemy, the modern liberal, who in his own way also prioritises an interpretive scheme based on a kind of humanly conceived non-negotiable certainty about what sort of thing the Bible is. The liberal scheme takes it for granted that there can be no such thing as writings which are 'the word of God' because those writings can be demonstrated to be the products of very human writers addressing the political, social and moral issues of their day, driven by struggles for influence and power within the communities they were a part of and for whom they wrote. Thus, the pastoral epistles (Timothy, Titus, etc) are 'really' about the arguments that must have been present in the early church about whether the church should be led and governed by bishops and priests, as opposed to the more prophetic and charismatic leadership model characteristic of the spontaneity of a 'Spirit led' community.

How then should we understand Holy Scripture, if it is not the 'word of God' as modelled on the 'inerrancy' principle on the one hand, nor simply a collection of expressions of the literary impulse in humankind to say something about the subject of God on the other?

If we take as our starting point the central Christian understanding that Jesus Christ is the Word of God and, as such, is the place where the encounter between God and humankind takes place, scripture can be seen as an auxiliary reality within that dynamic. In other words, God is He who has spoken to us 'by a Son'. This speaking is complete, all sufficient, and necessary as being graciously from God to us. But this is also the God who has 'spoken in many and various ways through the prophets', so that although the self-revelation of God in Christ is astonishingly new its newness is not that of novelty, or 'stand-alone' unlikeliness. Rather, it is the newness of fulfillment, the newness of full disclosure of that which had, until that unveiling, been somewhat hidden, or, we might say, that which had been muffled until its notes rang out in resounding clarity.

Therefore, the scriptures are not simply collections of spiritual wisdom or re-interpretations of conventional history given a theological twist as products of human enquiry and reflection. *They are the instrument that God employs in his self-revealing disclosure.* The writings themselves do indeed have an 'ordinary' provenance, in that they were written by men doing their writing in particular contexts, and they display all the marks of such origins, discernible as they are through their qualities of style, and the cross references they share with other historical accounts (e.g. the histories of empires, and their waxing and waning in the ancient Middle East).

Modern scholarship has revealed much more of this 'natural history' of the biblical texts than used to be available. This has furnished us with valuable material about the workings of the texts and their internal structure, so that when used reverentially, the clarity of God's word is enhanced. A good example of this kind of scholarship is the work that Dr Ken Bailey has done on the parables of Jesus in which he has sought to apply a full understanding of the cultural context in which they arose so that the impact of their meaning can be grasped by readers whose own cultural shaping is geographically, socially, and temporally different.

In Dr Bailey's analysis of the parable of the Prodigal Son, or, as we ought to say, The Two Sons, he reveals its extraordinary power by showing us how its first readers would have reacted to its telling. On the question of the younger son asking for his share of the inheritance Bailey used to ask people living in remote villages in the Levant, whose lives in those traditional societies were not so different from their forebears in the time of Jesus, what they thought of a son asking his perfectly healthy father for his share of the inheritance that would normally be his at his father's death.

Bailey says this:

'In the literally hundreds of times I have asked the question 'Do you know of anyone who has made such a request?' only twice did I receive an answer in the affirmative. The first occasion was reported by a pastor of Iranian extraction whose congregation was made up of converted Oriental Jews. One of his leading parishioners told him 'My son wants me to die!' The pastor discovered that the son had broached the topic of his inheritance. Three months later the father, despite being in apparently good health, died. The mother said 'He died that night' meaning, the night that the son had asked for his inheritance. The other occasion concerned a Syrian farmer whose son asked for his inheritance. In great anger his father drove him from the house.' *(Kenneth Bailey, 'Poet and Peasant', 1976, p162)*

The light shed by this kind of research provides rich reflective opportunities regarding what we could call the 'affront' to God that sin represents, and the whole subject of God's passibility, his apparent exposure to the effects of evil, and what that exposure costs him. It takes us much closer to the experience of hearing what Jesus meant, much deeper into the depth of meaning contained in the words themselves.

The issue then is not the fact that the scriptures have a 'natural history', which they clearly do, but whether having a natural history disqualifies them from being the instrument of God's voice. Such a disqualification can only be assumed if the old dualisms that we have already noticed a number of times, the dualisms of time and eternity, and of the material and the spiritual, intrude yet again. When they push their way into the subject of the understanding of scripture in the light of its 'natural history' they inevitably promote that natural provenance at the expense of any divine involvement. If you can trace the lineaments of the scripture's natural 'anatomy' you can confine scripture and its origins to the purely natural sphere, apparently.

In our unpicking of this false premise it is our turning again to the incarnation of 'he who is Son' and the illuminating work of the Holy Spirit, that floods our confusion with light. This is because the blind alley of the dualistic approach, which rejects any actual involvement by God in the business of history, and particularly the natural history of the scriptures, rests on a conception of God as an agency of causal will operating from outside the material realm of creation in the vacuum of his/her/its (?) remoteness. In complete contrast to this conception is the trinitarian reality of God, who acts towards and within his creation through the agency of his two hands (Irenaeus) – the Son and the Spirit, incorporating elements of the material and historical inventory of creation, such as human literary activity, into the divine self-disclosure made present in the Scriptures. Far from denying or down-grading the significance of the natural order (as exampled by the human authorship of the scriptures) such incorporating activity by God enables that element of the natural order, which is the human authorship of the scriptures, to manifest something of its divinely ordained destiny, which it shares with all creation, which is to glorify its creator, redeemer and perfecter.

Speaking of God's engagement with the natural order in this way, as we see it at work in the whole story of scripture's production, reminds us of an important 'mystery' in the working of the grace of God. Being taken up into the purposes of God by becoming a servant of his gracious will in this way might seem to indicate a kind of relegation of the natural order into a state of passivity, with overtones of the automaton, as if God's intimate involvement in the life of the natural must cause the natural to be overwhelmed by the supernatural, thereby losing some, if not all, of its individuality, particularity and freedom. The 'mystery' referred to above relates to what actually happens as a result of God's gracious and sovereign activity in and for the creature, which is that far from obliterating the distinctive creaturely reality of that which is taken up into God's purposes, that creaturely reality is enhanced, and advanced towards its perfecting. It becomes not less than what it is but more than what it is, or, more precisely, more fully approximated to the perfecting that is God's purpose for it. When we witness the Spirit at work in the life of a person whose life has been transformed by the indwelling presence of the triune God we find ourselves saying that this person is becoming *more* like their true self, *more* authentically free, because more completely a servant of their Lord *(2 Corinthians 3:17).*

In trying to lay bare what is really meant by saying that the Holy Scriptures are the 'word of God' we have tried to plot a path between two inadequate and dangerous over-simplifications. We have rejected the 'divinizing' of the text, in which it is claimed that the words of scripture are, in a literal sense, possessed of divine properties and therefore cannot exhibit any factual errors or contradictions. And we have rejected the opposite generalisation, which is to so emphasise the human origins and characteristics of the text that God is, by definition, excluded from any involvement in their production. Leaving the Scylla of divinizing on one side, and the Charybdis of naturalizing on the other, we are setting our course for an understanding of the word of God that can be defined as follows: God addresses us through the Holy Scriptures because they are *the servant of his Word's self-utterance.* (I owe this verbal formulation to Prof John Webster)

The chief advantage of this definition is that it preserves the priority of Christ as the Word of God in whom God's self-revelation consists, and it positions the scriptures in their correct relationship to the Word, which is to be auxiliary, taken into service, accorded their particular role, in being the vehicle through which the Word of God speaks to us.

This means that the essential activity of the church, the activity that defines the church as the people of God, is listening to the Holy Scriptures so that the church may hear what the Word of God says. That is why the reading of Holy Scripture is the centrepiece of Christian worship, even eucharistic worship (which is, in fact, replete with biblical quotations and references), because it is in the hearing of its words that we hear the Word – we hear Jesus, who is nothing less than the self-utterance of God in our midst. This is the point that we met in Chapter 1 (Time) when we noted that vision comes a very distant second to hearing as the primary sense through which we encounter God's engagement with us.

Therefore, Holy Scripture, because it is the servant of the self-utterance of God who is the Word is not a kind of Christian comfort blanket, at our disposal to protect us from hard truths, nor a weapon to be used in disputes with other Christians, nor a collection of spiritual masterpieces like arrows in a quiver. In all those ways of using scripture it is we who are in control. We deploy it to our own ends. No. Holy Scripture is simply where we hear the voice of the Word of God, Jesus Christ himself.

If you asked most Christians, especially Christians who love their Bibles, to pick a metaphor for the gracious words of Jesus that come to them intimately and savingly as they read, they would, perhaps, choose something like 'a gold coin' (precious, costly, beautiful), or 'a love letter' (intimate, personal, affirming,). But Holy Scripture's own metaphor for the gracious words of the Word is, 'sharp two-edged sword' *('...the word of God is living and active, sharper than any two-edged sword...' Hebrews 4:12)*. Left to ourselves it would never occur to us to use such an image. It's much too threatening, too military even. To use a modern idiom, it seems to weaponize Jesus' voice.

But if we take seriously the Christian conviction that God the Holy Spirit has providentially enabled the Holy Scriptures to be what they are, the self-utterance of God's Word, it seems that we must ditch our own glowingly comfortable metaphors and accept the one that God himself has used.

When we hear the words of scripture, by which we mean when we hear the self-utterance of the Word of God, we should expect to feel its sharpness, its truth telling, its exposure of our pretence, its dismantling of our self-regarding spirituality. If that sword has done its job there will be blood on the floor, the result of the destruction of the false self that we tried to hide behind when God came calling, when the voice like a trumpet sounded like many waters from the Living One in our midst *(Revelation 1:15).* In his examination of what Bonhoeffer has to say about the scriptures John Webster has this to say, speaking of our encounter with the Word who speaks through the scriptures:

'Moreover, what we encounter in that revelation is not some satisfying extension of our previous selves, but rather something strange and disagreeable, for (quoting Bonhoeffer) 'if it is God who says where he will be, than that will truly be a place which at first sight is not agreeable to me, which does not fit so well with me. That place is the cross of Christ,' *(John Webster, 'Holy Scripture, a Dogmatic Sketch', p85)*

Thinking about metaphors (gold coins, love letters, sharp two-edged swords etc) leads us on to a different kind of meditation concerning words and their role in our knowledge of God. So far, we have carried out our task using the tools of analysis and exegesis. To put that metaphorically, we have behaved like scientists performing a dissection, with the Bible pinned open on the dissection slab. There is nothing wrong with such an approach, but it is by no means the only, nor even necessarily the best, way to discover the connection between words and the Truth.

In the main section of the first chapter of the Book of Revelation (i.e. verses 4 – 20) there are seventeen vivid metaphors ('hair white as wool', 'eyes...like a flame of fire'), most of them used in reference to the risen Jesus, depicted as addressing, from within their midst, the seven churches of Asia who are the recipients of John's revelation. Neither the Book of Revelation as a whole, nor chapter one in particular, are poems as such, yet in many respects they are poetic rather than prosaic in nature. They employ strikingly vivid imagery. They are not so much an engineer's plan of how things are, but an artist's brightly coloured, impressionistic canvas depicting reality in all its beauty. Not a line drawing diagram of how to put together a model aeroplane, but a Monet landscape of poppies in a summer cornfield, or a wind-fluttered parasol against an azure sky.

In her introduction to a selection of George Herbert's writings the poet Wendy Cope describes how Herbert's spiritual poetry played its part in her return to churchgoing. In celebrating Herbert's genius she touches on his technical achievements and his playfulness, rejecting the accusation that Herbert might be simply an accomplished verbal technician whose 'light' style betrays a lack of seriousness. She affirms Herbert as a serious poet, 'whose primary concern was not to show off, but to tell the truth.' *(Wendy Cope, 'George Herbert, Verse and Prose' pxiii)*

In our consideration of how the Holy Scriptures should be understood as 'the word of God' we took an analytical approach. As part of that process, we noted that in our reading of the scriptures the Holy Spirit is able to undertake his work of sanctification and perfecting in the reader, and that the 'traffic of attention' therefore is by no means all in the direction of reader towards the written word, but is, in an important sense, from written word to reader. The scripture reads us as much as we read it. Here is how George Herbert clothes this idea, speaking of the scriptures:

Thou art all health, health thriving till it make

A full eternitie: thou art a masse

Of strange delights, where we may wish and take.

Ladies, look here; this is the thankfull glasse,

That mends the lookers eyes: this is the well

That washes what it shows.

(George Herbert, 'The H. Scriptures 1', lines 5 – 11)

The complex dynamics at work between the reader and the words being read are captured in just nine words ('...this is the well That washes what it shows'), words which carry a wealth of meaning borne on the dense interplay of ideas associated with looking, mirroring, washing and refreshing that are present in the act of looking down a well at the water deep within it.

The first part of the poem then ends with the following lines, still speaking, of course, of the Holy Scriptures:

Thou art joyes handsell: heav'n lies flat in thee,

Subject to ev'ry mounters bended knee.

In our contrasting of the analytical approach and the poetic approach we used the image of the Bible being pinned open on the dissection slab subject to the scientist's scalpel. Herbert employed a similar picture nearly 300 years before we got there (!) employing the image of the scriptures lying open, flat before us, thereby opening heaven itself to our gaze – a much more positive scenario. More than this, Herbert goes on to a depiction of the scriptures' passivity in allowing themselves to be so interrogated, but only by those who are prepared to approach them on 'bended knee' i.e in an attitude of prayer.

In our chapter on 'Time' we engaged with important questions to do with temporality, eternity, our material existence, and our gropings towards the transcendent. That involved, naturally, some assessment of philosophical approaches to such questions, especially those of Plato and Kant. We saw how the Christian approach to these apparent dualities takes a radically different course, using the Incarnation as its lens onto reality, and what that means for the human condition (to use the term coined influentially by Hannah Arendt). Philosophy tends to be unavoidably speculative and individually conceived. These qualities do not necessarily undermine philosophy's usefulness, but they do draw attention to its tendency to float free of the nitty-gritty of ordinary human existence, with its mundane necessities and its short attention span. In his poem 'The Agonie' Herbert, without belittling philosophy, wrests our attention away from cosmic speculation towards more urgent concerns that the human condition throws up:

> Philosophers have measur'd the mountains,
> Fathom'd the depths of the seas, of states, and kings,
> Walk'd with a staffe to heav'n, and traced fountains:
> But there are two vast, spacious things,

> The which to measure it doth more behove:
> Yet few there are that found them; Sinne and Love.
>
>   Who would know Sinne, let him repair
> Unto mount Olivet; there shall he see
> A man so wrung with pains, that all his hair,
>   His skinne, his garments bloudie be.
> Sinne is that presse and vice, which forceth pain
> To hunt his cruell food through ev'ry vein.
>
>   Who knows not Love, let him assay,
> And taste that juice, which on the crosse a pike
> Did set again abroach; then let him say
>   If ever he did taste the like.
> Love is that liquor sweet and most divine,
> Which my God feels as bloude; but I, as wine.
>
> *(George Herbert, 'The Agonie')*

Theological theories about exactly how Christ's death deals with the sin of the world take a variety of forms and employ a variety of metaphorical devices. These include the law court (the acceptance of a judicial judgement on sin; Rom 3:19 - 26), the ransoming of a captive or slave (Eph 1:7) and the idea of substitution, where Christ accepts on our behalf the punishment that is due to us all (Rom 8:32).

'The Agonie' suggests that although natural curiosity and human affairs present us with big questions that stretch our intellectual capacities to, and perhaps beyond, their limits, any achievements in the sphere of knowledge *per se* are dwarfed by the urgency of matters that lie much closer to home: the realities of sin and love, universal realities, which constitute the essence of the human condition.

One way of confirming how sin and love account for most of what matters in a human life is to take a biography, and then excise from it anything of that life which could be identified as having come about by the impact of either of these two fundamental human experiences on the person concerned (e.g. via their parents, friends, enemies, colleagues etc), or by the actions of the subject of the biography which stemmed from their own sinful or loving impulses directed towards others. In most cases the resulting volume would be very thin indeed.

Only a decade or two before Herbert wrote 'The Agonie' the Dutch artist Hieronymus Wierix produced an engraving which happens to be a depiction of the meaning of the poem's second and third verses. It shows Jesus standing in a large vat, as was used in a winepress. He is bent over with the weight of the cross which bears down on his shoulders. As a result, the 'juice' of his blood is squeezed from his body, to become the 'wine' that fills the vat, the wine that is the blood of Christ. The image is, fundamentally, a diagrammatic representation of an idea, and as such it is somewhat unsatisfactory because it replaces in our minds a picture of what the crucifixion probably looked like with a manifestly non-representational image which is more slogan than icon, more sermon than portrait. It is not just personal taste that places Herbert's words on a higher plane of piety and insight than this engraving. It is their power to draw us in to what is happening by imagining ourselves to be at the foot of that cross as witness and perpetrator (through our sin) that makes them ring true:

Sinne is that presse and vice, which forceth pain

To hunt his cruell food through ev'ry vein.

The connections between sin and pain are too numerous to count, and too obvious to describe. The pain endured by Christ is easily correlated with sin. Love is less easy to render in terms of a cause or product, being, as it is commonly understood, an emotion experienced more or less passively, especially in our own times, when love is often taken to be only about feelings. But Herbert sees that in fact the connection between pain/sin and love is manifested by Christ's blood, which is not simply the plain by-product of nails, spear and thorns, but is the currency of love itself, the measure of his self-giving.

The third verse invites an even more dramatic self-involvement in the scene than does the second, in that it pictures us not merely gazing in wonder but leaning forwards to allow the flowing blood to find its way into our open mouths, so that we find ourselves, in our imaginations, enacting literally what we do figuratively each time we drink the wine of the eucharist/mass/communion. The Christian church has argued, on and off, for nearly two thousand years about exactly how the wine of the eucharist is in fact the blood of Christ. Herbert rejects, by inference, all the convoluted and abstruse arguments of the theologians and ecclesiastics. It is not ontology, or metaphysics, or any kind of gnostic alchemy that gives us the way in to what is happening in the eucharist. Better than all that mental effort is the sensual extravagance, the intoxicating pleasure, brought on by the tasting and swallowing of that best of all wines, the elixir of life:

Who knows not Love, let him assay,

And taste that juice,…..

Love is that liquor sweet and most divine,

Which my God feels as bloude: but I, as wine.

In his poem 'Judgement' Herbert continues his exploration of the connection between our sin and Christ's vicarious death. He builds his meditation around the comparison that can be made between the idea of a person's life being described as a 'book', with its pages telling the life-story in question, and the book of the scriptures (he uses the term 'Testament') which tell the 'life-story' of salvation.

Almightie Judge, how shall poore wretches brook
        Thy dreadfull look,
Able a heart of iron to appall,
        When thou shalt call
  For ev'ry man's peculiar book?

What others mean to do, I know not well;
        Yet I heare tell,
That some will turn thee to some leaves therein
        So void of sinne,
  That they in merit shall excell.

But I resolve, when thou shalt call for mine,
        That to decline,
And thrust a Testament into thy hand:
        Let that be scann'd.
  There thou shalt finde my faults are thine. *(George Herbert, 'Judgement)*

Lurking just under the surface of Herbert's actual lines is the idea that the true outline and contours of a person's life are not visible from an earthly perspective but only from the heavenly. Only God knows what the outcome would be when any particular life is measured in the balances, because only God knows everything that there is to be known about any life. This is why human judgementalism (a very popular pastime these days) is such a dangerous sin, because it amounts to putting oneself in the place of God. From God's viewpoint there is no such thing as a person's 'life-book,' taken by itself, as if it tells the whole story of that life. This is because no human life exists outside of the deeper reality which is God's human life in Christ. Christ's life is the lens through which God looks at every human life, because humanity exists only in the light cast by the Second Adam, and that shining is not a mere high-point of history alongside other major events, about which we might have arguments as to its ranking in relation to those other events. It is the Event which makes any other event possible *(Ephesians 1: 4 – 10, Colossians 1: 15 – 17).*

Herbert's take on this idea is drawn straightforwardly enough as, for the sake of his poetic aim, he accepts the idea of a person's 'book', but only so that he can set the scene for his daring final line. Most sons know what it means to say that some of their personal faults can be seen to be their father's, in the sense that they are not new. They are just a reprise brought about by genes and unfortunate imitation. Herbert's daring is to take this human characteristic so that it can be re-drawn in the light of the New Testament, and its account of God taking to himself our faults, so that they become no longer ours, but his, on the cross.

I have chosen to focus on George Herbert as an example of how poetry can be more effective than prose in its use of words to describe truths about God (and ourselves) not because he is the only poet with something to say about God, but because he is, to some extent, familiar to anyone who has sung hymns ('Let all the world in every corner sing….' etc.), and because his work is such a wonderful example of Samuel Taylor Coleridge's assessment of poetry as 'the best words in the best order.'

It is also important to stress that the poetic is not limited to poetry. This is an especially important point when we acknowledge that many people have no instinctive liking of poetry, and may well be put off poetry by uncomfortable memories of dull English lessons at school.

As we saw with the Book of Revelation there are numerous places in the scripture where ideas are expressed poetically without the passage in question being itself a poem. This is partly due to the way in which metaphor (a figure of speech applied to something non-literally, thereby illuminating meaning through a comparison) functions not as a piece of optional literary decoration, like a flower in a bride's hair, but more like the carefully constructed network of grips and pins which hold the hairdresser's creation together. Metaphors are in fact an essential component in the toolbox of techniques that we use to describe not just what we already know, but what we are feeling our way towards knowing. They act like stepping stones in the process that takes place when we move from knowledge that we already have, to knowledge not yet fully grasped. It is also because statements about non-physical realities (like love, faith, trust etc) become more meaningful when physical things or familiar ideas are attached to them for the sake of descriptive depth and verisimilitude, as in 'I am the Good Shepherd' (i.e. the one who can be trusted) or 'we are the clay, you are our potter' *(Isaiah 64:8)* (i.e. God fashions us into something useful, or even beautiful, despite the fact that we are unpromising material until he works on us). Irenaeus' analogy for the Son and the Spirit being the 'two hands' of God is a good example of a metaphor opening up meaning where non-metaphorical (i.e. literal, direct) speech is inappropriate, or cumbersome, or indeed more or less impossible (given that, in this case, the subject is the Holy Trinity).

We have already made reference to Herbert's poem 'The H. Scriptures'. The lines we used come from Part 1 of the poem. Part 2 moves to an aspect of the reading of scripture that has often been noted which is that scripture is its own best interpreter. This is the idea that any particular verse may have light shed on its meaning by another verse elsewhere in the Bible that deals with the same or a similar subject. Herbert puts it like this:

Oh that I knew how all thy lights combine,
    And the configurations of their glorie!
    Seeing not onely how each verse doth shine,
But all the constellations of the storie.

This verse marks that, and both do make a motion
    Unto a third, that ten leaves off doth lie:
    Then as dispersed herbs do watch a potion,
These three make up some Christians destinie:

Such are thy secrets, which my life makes good,
    And comments on thee: for in ev'ry thing

> Thy words do finde me out, & parallels bring,
> And in another make me understood.
>
> > Starres are poore books, & oftentimes do misse:
> > This book of starres lights to eternall blisse.

(George Herbert, 'H.Scriptures 2')

It is sometimes claimed that because the Bible is a collection of writings by many different authors who lived at various times within a total span of about 700 years it can have no single 'voice', in the sense of having a unity of theme. The second verse of Part 2 of 'The H(oly) Scriptures' stands as the answer to this claim in its testimony, born of experience, an experience echoed by countless readers of the Scriptures over the ages. Closely associated with this idea about the interconnectedness of biblical ideas and their multiple anchorings in different types of writings within the biblical whole is the way in which a train of thought leading to new insight can be triggered by mere word association. The starting point is not a sentence or sentences found in a verse (as described by the second verse of 'The H. Scriptures' part 2), but a single word.

In our chapter 2 ('Nature') we noted how the word 'garden' can work like this in the biblical context, drawing us into meditations on major biblical ideas like The Fall (the Garden of Eden), the humanity of Christ (the Garden of Gethsemane) and the resurrection of Christ (the Resurrection Garden). We also noted in that discussion that gardens feature as a metaphor for paradise and perfection in many religious traditions. The power of association triggered by a single word may well extend beyond the biblical text itself and into the thought world of the reader in ways that appear to be instinctive and subconscious.

A colleague of mine recounted to me the following story of a young woman in the congregation he was serving in Cambridge in the 1980s. The young woman was Japanese. While following her course of study in Cambridge she became interested in Christianity. In due course she became a Christian. Her parents, siblings, and the whole wider family back in Japan were shocked and troubled by her conversion, despite the fact that they could not deny the reality of her new-found joy and peace. How could she abandon her culture, her beliefs, her family, her future? And why hem herself in to a restrictive, controlling, and alien belief system? 'You are making yourself a prisoner inside a high-walled prison' they said.

'Yes,' she said. 'I am now living within a walled space, but the space is a garden, surrounded by a high wall – a walled garden. But here's the strange thing. Every time I walk from the centre of the garden towards one of the walls, I never reach the wall. It always retreats away from me, opening up ever greater space in the garden itself, so that the garden is constantly expanding. The space in which I live as a Christian is protected space, protected by Christ, and it is limitless space, made limitless by the freedom I have in Christ.'

I don't know what her family's response was to this beautiful, poetic (and very Japanese!) testimony. But as an example of the power of words sanctified and energized by the Spirit in the task of explaining the experience of being 'in Christ', it is without parallel in my experience.

Person

Our family summer holidays in the 1980s usually took the form of camping near the French Atlantic coast. The family memory archive from that decade is dominated by a kaleidoscope of sights, sounds and smells made up of breezy skies, salty spray, children's excited squealing mixed with seagulls' squawking, and the sweet, gritty woad of melting ice cream smeared carelessly on sandy skin.

But my own memories of those holidays are anchored to an event that fixed those personal experiences to the wider sweep of history itself. It was while driving back to the Channel coast ferry that we heard on the radio news that the borders of Hungary were starting to show signs of disintegration as brave and desperate Hungarian citizens made their way tentatively over the crossings to Austria, gaining a taste of the freedom which the communist system had denied them for so long. Within weeks the citizens of East Germany and Czechoslovakia followed suit. A short time later the Berlin Wall had fallen.

For anyone born after about 1950 there are a few events from history that qualify for a very exclusive collection defined by the preamble 'Where were you when you heard the news that....?' Alongside the collapse of Soviet controlled communism would be the assassination of John F Kennedy, the landing of the first man on the moon, and, perhaps, the attack on the twin Trade Center towers on 9/11.

The collapse of Soviet communism carries a weight of historical significance that needs little elaboration from a geo-political perspective. What gives those events of the late 1980s and early 1990s a universal poignancy deeper than mere politics and ideology is the way in which we saw in them a basic human aspiration playing out.

In his passionate analysis of the truth about life lived under the suffocating ideology of the Soviet system as it took its form in Czechoslovakia Vaclav Havel described how even an ideology built on a lie could have a kind of bogus attraction through offering something 'high', a cause to unite behind:

'Ideology is a specious way of relating to the world. It offers human beings the illusion of an identity, of dignity, and of morality while making it easier for them to *part* with them.' *(Vaclav Havel, 'The Power of the Powerless' p16)*

He proceeds to a description of the needs and desires that characterise human life when the individual person is free to engage with the world as it actually is, and not as it is artificially constructed by the imposition of an ideology:

'The essential aims of life are present naturally in every person. In everyone there is some longing for humanity's rightful dignity, for moral integrity, for free expression of being and a sense of transcendence over the world of existences. Yet, at the same time, each person is capable, to a greater or lesser degree, of coming to terms with living within the lie. Each person somehow succumbs to a profane trivialization of his or her inherent humanity, and to utilitarianism. In everyone there is some willingness to merge with the anonymous crowd and to flow comfortably along with it down the river of pseudo-life. This is much more than a simple conflict between two identities. It is something far worse: it is a challenge to the very notion of identity itself.' *(Huvel, p34 – 35)*

What makes Havel's analysis so compelling is its honesty, and its anchoring in the granite-like certainties of actual human experience. A single sentence taken from the furnace of his own crucible of reflection is worth whole chapters taken from philosophical and anthropological speculations produced in the quiet leather-bound ambience of a university library. Not only does he pinpoint humanity's unquenchable longing for 'freedom', but he also confronts us with our susceptibility to the apparent attractions of that which imprisons, that which diminishes us, that behind which we can hide from the truth. He takes us to the heart of the conundrum of human existence itself and what we might make of what we call the 'person', the thing of which each of us is an example, the thing which attracts admiration or disgust in equal measure. Pascal described our puzzling propensity for both good and evil with blunt honesty in describing the human creature as being 'the glory and refuse of the universe'.

Critics of religion have often taken the Bible to be an instrument of oppression, an example of something which seeks to prevent mankind (humankind) from achieving its 'coming of age'. Those critics would probably be surprised to learn that the Bible's view of humanity is as positive as it is. When the Psalmist reflected on the enigma of humanity, he concluded that humanity was not enigmatic on account of its patchy record of righteousness so much as on its exalted status within the cosmic purposes of the Creator:

What is man, that thou art mindful of him? and the son of man, that thou visitest him?
For thou hast made him a little lower than the angels, and hast crowned him with glory and honour.
Thou madest him to have dominion over the works of thy hands; thou hast put all things under his feet:
all sheep and oxen, yea, and the beasts of the field;
The fowl of the air, and the fish of the sea, and whatsoever passeth through the paths of the seas. *(Psalm 8: 4 – 8, KJV)*

There is more than a hint of Psalm 8 in Shakespeare's own portrayal of the creature who delights and exasperates in equal measure:

> What a piece of work is a man, how noble in reason, how infinite in faculties, in form and moving how express and admirable, in action how like an angel, in apprehension how like a god: the beauty of the world, the paragon of animals! And yet to me what is this quintessence of dust? Man delights not me – nor woman neither, though by your smiling you seem to say so. *(Hamlet, Act 2, scene 2)*

With these thoughts and sketchings we are embarking on our consideration of what Christian believing and living has to say about the subject of the person. A moment's reflection reveals that the term takes us beyond the idea of mere 'human being'. If we limit ourselves to 'human being' we are thinking of the subject at the simple biological level. Both the psalmist and Shakespeare are clearly delving far deeper into the idea of 'man' ('humankind') than the fact that he has animal existence, notwithstanding Shakespeare's reference to his being 'the paragon of animals'. Havel's comments about 'longing', 'transcendence' and 'free expression of being' strike a chord, and we recognize straight away that he is talking about the infinitely more complex and puzzling phenomenon that we call the life of a man or woman as it takes place from birth to death alongside the lives of many others, well known to him or her, as well as lesser known.

Very close to the centre of what we think a person is must be the matter of freedom. Animals have little freedom in the sense that their lives are shaped by very basic requirements and instincts. If some of the higher animals exercise choice (after a fashion) their choosing is very rudimentary and almost always from a very limited set of possibilities. By contrast, human beings can conceptualize a wide range of potential scenarios that could unfold from any given point in time, depending on a range of possible inputs, each of which might demand a different kind of response, leading in turn to yet another range of options requiring further consideration and planned action. All of that weighing up of possibilities and probabilities takes place within a mental world that is open to a realistic appreciation of the possibilities inherent in the future. Once we sketch out the territory in this way we start to see how vastly different human experience is from that of the rest of the animal kingdom.

When we try to depict the drama of human life like this we can also see how our understanding of ourselves as persons is affected by our understanding of the setting we find ourselves in. How we answer questions about the world, its origin and its purpose, will affect how we answer questions about ourselves. Christian ideas about the person therefore are profoundly influenced by Christian ideas about God, who is the creator, sustainer and perfecter of all things. We will come, in due course, to an engagement with this theology.

But because we do not live in a hermetically sealed Christian enclave, unaffected by alternative ideas and beliefs, it will be useful to attempt an assessment of the ideas that swirl around us regarding these big questions, especially the question of human freedom. As we have seen with our glance at the fall of Soviet communism freedom lies at the heart of the debates which ebb and flow about the most fundamental questions concerning social organization and individual fulfillment. Alongside the struggles in Eastern Europe and Russia we could place the equally dramatic story of South Africa. 'Cry Freedom' was surely the easiest choice of title for Richard Attenborough's film about apartheid.

It is not difficult to portray the challenges which confront human life through the lens of large scale political and social realities (like the collapse of Soviet communism, or the persistent stain on communal life of dictatorship as an example of social and political organisation). Important as these major historical realities are it would be misleading to suggest that they account for the experiences of freedom (or its absence) in the lives of all people. Neither do the courageous and insightful responses of people like Vaclav Havel give us a complete picture of the ways that modern people frame their personal ambitions and hopes for a fulfilling life. This is especially true for the many people who enjoy the political freedoms that modern democracies provide, underpinned as those democracies are by an axiomatic belief that the individual person should be free to pursue their own vision of self-fulfillment. Here is an early example of what the 'personal fulfillment industry' has produced in response to the perceived market demand for direction towards the achievement of a satisfying experience of modern selfhood:

'Be gentle with yourself. You are a child of the Universe no less than the trees and stars. You have a right to be here. And whether or not it is clear to you, no doubt the universe is unfolding as it should. Therefore be at peace with God, whatever you conceive Him to be. And whatever your labors and aspirations, in the noisy confusion of life, keep peace in your soul. With all its sham, drudgery and broken dreams, it is still a beautiful world.' *(Robert Bellah, 'Habits of the Heart', 1985)*

There are many criticisms that might be made of such a philosophy (and the numerous other and similar examples that could be quoted). It is enough for now to note just two things.

The first is the assumption that it is the individual person who has the right and responsibility to fashion their own response to the challenges of life according to their own felt needs ('be gentle with yourself….keep peace in your soul….'). The second is that despite a reference to 'God', which gives the impression of there being a transcendent dimension to life, the conviction about the divine in this philosophy is that it is a psychological rather than a transcendent reality. 'God' is 'whatever you conceive Him to be', which ties Him irrevocably to the limited scope defined by my own experience and imagination. This God cannot avoid being merely the best version of myself that I can imagine.

Although the word 'feel' does not crop up in this quoted example there is no doubt that feelings represent the litmus test of any modern philosophy of life. It is not just the triumphant and out of breath sportsman or woman being interviewed who gets asked 'How do you feel?' In a sense we all get asked that question all the time by the culture that places the arena of validation in the interior life, having transferred it there from the realm of objective and exterior realities. This is the phenomenon noticed by Matthew Syed which we quoted in the Preface.

In his magisterial account *('Sources of the Self', Harvard Univ Press, 1989)* of how modern understandings of the self have evolved into what they are today Charles Taylor highlights this move from the objective exterior to the subjective interior as a defining feature of contemporary anthropology in a Western perspective. He quotes the Austrian poet Rainer Maria Rilke:

'Nowhere, beloved, will world be, but within us. Our life
passes in transformation. And the external

shrinks into less and less. Where once an enduring house was,
now a cerebral structure crosses our path, completely
belonging to the realm of concepts, as though it stood still in the
brain....
Where one of them still survives,
a Thing that was formerly prayed to, worshipped, knelt before-
just as it is, it passes into the invisible world.

('The Selected Poetry of Rainer Maria Rilke', 1984)

Perhaps it is inevitable that the focus of life should shift to the interior, and the seemingly endless process of reflection on the self, in the wake of the rejection of God who is the transcendent 'other', who by his providential ordering of the created realm ensures its significance and its movement towards becoming perfected. Without that over-arching context human life has nowhere else to turn than back on itself. It is in this context that the rise of 'therapy' can be explained in the modern world, as an indicator of the need for answers to the big questions of life where the locus for such answers can no longer be the exterior and the transcendent and must therefore be the interior and the imminent.

There is a kind of rough and ready wisdom about attending to one's own felt needs before anything else, justified, after a fashion, by the thought that we might be of better use to others once we have done all that we need to do to make of ourselves all that we can. The reality is, of course, that we never reach the point at which we acknowledge that we are now fit 'for others'. There is always something more that we ourselves apparently need. Dorothy L Sayers, in characteristically straightforward fashion, points us to where this prioritizing of the self ultimately leads:

'If we refuse assent to reality; if we rebel against the nature of things and choose to think that what we at the moment want is the centre of the universe to which everything else ought to accommodate itself, the first effect on us will be that the whole universe will seem to be filled with an implacable and inexplicable hostility. We shall begin to feel that everything has a down on us, and that, being so badly treated, we have a just grievance against things in general. That is the knowledge of good as evil and the fall into illusion. If we cherish and fondle that grievance, and would rather wallow in it, and vent our irritation in spite and malice than humbly admit that we are in the wrong and try to amend our behaviour so as to get back to reality, that is, while it lasts, the deliberate choice, and a foretaste of the experience, of hell.' *(Dorothy L Sayers, 'Introductory Papers on Dante', Vol 1, p 64)*

Despite the fact that Sayers wrote that in the 1940s it is not difficult to see how it could be not only an insight into human nature in general but also a commentary on the modern phenomenon of aggressive activism, in which righteous indignation turns so often into toxic condemnation. Instead of producing 'light-bulb' moments of perception and cooperation it leads, more usually, to a desire for violent reaction and further polarization.

The Slovenian philosopher and social commentator Slajov Zizek is not everyone's cup of tea, but he is surely onto something in his highlighting of self-absorption as a defining characteristic of modern life, and the way in which this carries with it a certain inner contradiction:

The basic characteristic of today's subjectivity is the weird combination of the free subject who experiences himself as ultimately responsible for his fate, and the subject who grounds the authority of his speech on his status of a victim of circumstances beyond his control... The notion of subject as a victim involves the extreme narcissistic perspective: every encounter with the Other appears as a potential threat to the subject's precarious imaginary balance. *(Quoted by Stephen Poole, The Spectator, 13.8.22)*

Along with that loss of the significance of the exterior goes also the loss of purpose and ambition directed towards the needs of others who in fact represent competition for the attention of the person on their way to self-realization. The concept of self-sacrifice, and even the heroic, becomes incomprehensible when the self is dedicated to what Nietzsche called 'pitiable comfort' – the rejection of a life of self-denial for the sake of a greater good, in favour of a life of self-absorption for the sake of ease. This begs the question: 'What place can there be in such an atmosphere for a faith that has self-sacrifice writ large at its very centre?'

This is a bleak assessment of the troubling loss of purpose that seems to characterize much of modern life, even though individual examples can always be found of lives that hold on to the reality of the 'exterior', thereby bucking the trend. The apparent competition between the 'exterior' and the 'interior' (a classically Kantian bifurcation) for ownership of the primary realm of reality encapsulates much of the confusion that gives modern life its distinctive feel, in which the individual must plough their way through thickets of varied and competing accounts of life and its purpose, expressed in the contexts of daily interaction with others, and in the strident assertions that fill the ether of social media. This is the bewilderingly varied and restless landscape of contemporary modernism (or post-modernism) in which no culture or 'lived experience' is allowed to be inferior or superior to any other, but where a vestige of universal and unavoidable truth is still accorded to science, or as we have noted several times, 'scientism'. It is worth looking at some of the story of how science has come to occupy the place that it has in the modernist culture that still reveres science's success, while also embracing cultural relativism whose energies sometimes appear to pull in the opposite direction.

A major feature of the phenomenon known as the Enlightenment was its conviction that the advances being made in scientific discovery which had followed on apace from the Copernican revolution were consolidating a new awakening in humankind's understanding of the world and humanity's part in it. Following in the wake of Copernicus, Kepler, Galileo, Newton, and others, enquiry about the natural world could proceed on the basis of observation, experimentation and consequent deduction. This brought about a profound shift of 'epistemological allegiance'; from theorizing about the world on the basis of philosophical and religious convictions, (e.g. the earth must be at the centre of everything because that is where God became part of his creation) to proofs about the world on the basis of what we now recognise as the scientific method. It is not too much of an exaggeration to say that the high priesthood of knowledge passed from the caste of priests to the community of scientists. There is no question now that it is to the scientific community that we look when seeking answers to our problems, both on the macro (social) and micro (individual) scale. This passing of authority from one community to another is clearly enough seen with hindsight, but it is worth noting in passing that there was considerable overlap during the gradual change. Much of the pioneering scientific effort put in by heroic, or even idiosyncratic, amateur (amateur in the sense of 'spare time') scientists in the eighteenth and nineteenth centuries was carried out by priests. The strict divide in the popular mind between 'scientific person' and 'religious person', is, of course, completely false. The picture of a Church of England parson collecting specimens or conducting botanical experiments during his untroubled afternoons is the stuff of caricature, but it is based on plenty of real-life examples (e.g. Rev'd Gilbert White, naturalist and pioneering ecologist).

Despite the evident theological motivation that many of these eighteenth and nineteenth century scientists had because of their convictions about the Author of nature and the beauty of his designs, it was perhaps inevitable that as the human capacity for understanding based on measurement and observation grew, so did the implicit belief that God was no longer needed as the great Explainer. The story of the decline of Christian belief in Europe and the West is not accounted for only by this dynamic, but it was certainly a significant element in that great change.

For the controversialists and the iconoclasts, it seemed obvious that humankind was entering a promised land of virtually limitless human agency directed towards the mastery of its environment. All this had become possible, apparently, through casting off the old constraints of superstition and ecclesiastical control. The implications for an understanding of the person seemed obvious. Humankind was starting to enter an era of freedom, and the individual person took 'freedom' to mean the opportunity, or even the right, to live life in a kind of vacuum, a space from which constraints, especially those perceived to be imposed by previously discredited authorities (the church, tradition etc), had been removed.

Some champions of the new 'freedom' took the idea of individual autonomy and choice to its logical conclusion by treating all external determining factors of choice (e.g. societal norms, education, tradition etc) as denials of freedom, and therefore as targets of revision or dissolution. It is not difficult to see that modern assumptions about the nature of personal freedom are simply the further development and extension of these ideas, so that 'freedom,' as it relates to a person, means the absence of constraint. Life, in this ideal, is lived in a void.

In practice, of course, the notion of the void is impossible to maintain. No-one lives life as if they are in a bubble within which every action and choice is carried out as if it were fashioned on a pristine, blank slate. To paraphrase a well-known saying of Jesus in which he spoke of the exorcised unclean spirit:

'When the unclean spirit has gone out of a person it wanders through waterless regions…Then it says 'I will return to my house from which I came.' Then it goes and brings along seven other spirits more evil than itself, and they enter and live there….' *(Matt 12: 43 – 45)*

In reality, the idea of the 'void' plays out against a background of scientism in society at large, in which it is assumed that everything can be explained mechanistically. Once we have a complete knowledge, via 'science', of things as they are in the present and past, based on a complete knowledge of the chains of cause and effect, we will be able to predict the future with complete accuracy. The irony is that explicatory success of this mechanistic sort leads to the loss of the freedom we thought we had won. Certain knowledge of the future on the basis of a complete understanding of the mechanisms that produced the present leads to determinism – the removal of free will itself, so that we end up being de-personalized, wandering through life like zombified automatons, prevented by a certain future from making choices, and therefore not released into, but deprived of, personal freedom. To banish

God from the public forum of debate about how we should live, and to imagine that the space created is empty and pristine, is, to employ the gospel metaphor, to sweep the house clean only for seven other unclean spirits to come in its place. In modern Western life those spirits take many forms, but among them are simplistic versions of 'nature', or 'evolution', or 'cosmic consciousness' or 'radical materialism'. As G K Chesterton is reputed to have said, 'When people stop believing in God, they do not believe in nothing. They believe in anything.'

It is interesting that the two ends of the 'freedom spectrum' (absolute freedom, as in the 'void' idea, and absolute determinism, as in the mechanistic/scientism model) tend to turn into one another, as we have sketched in the brief discussion above. That this leads not merely to post-prandial, port-fueled, discussion but real-life consequences becomes apparent when we notice that scientific determinism, as with Soviet ideology and policy, and some forms of technocratic societal control (e.g. through the tight control of electronic communication) usually results in a form of dystopia in society, along the lines set out by Vaclav Havel. As Edward Craig has put it in his criticism of scientific and ideological determinism:

[Scientific or ideological determinism] is psychologically unstable in itself. It is the philosophy of the confident man, or, as its opponents would very likely have it, the over-confident man. Should that confidence flag it offers no secure consolation. The image of the void, from being a symbol of limitless liberty of the agent, becomes a menacing abyss waiting to engulf all his purposes and reduce him to a nullity.' *(Edward Craig, 'The Mind of God and the Works of Man', 1987, p271)*

If, for the time being, we stick with the approach to 'freedom' that we find in modern Western ways of thinking, we can see that it is predicated on a conception of the person as a fully formed consciousness facing, or confronting, the universe as it finds it, deploying its powers of reason and analysis as it tries to make sense of it, from within an individualistic paradigm in which the single person is master, judge and jury.

The enormous weakness of this model is its proposal that the person is in fact a completely independent, solitary agent of choice and action. The reality is that persons are what they are as persons because they live in relation with other persons, for good or ill, and with everything else, including, from the Christian viewpoint, God.

This truth about personhood being a relational reality and not an existentially singular (individualistic) reality can be demonstrated as soon as we contemplate the concept of a person being cloned (horror of horrors). The creation in a laboratory of a replication of a particular human being in a biological or bodily sense may well be possible in the not-so-distant future. Assuming that the creature so 'created' is an exact genetic copy of an existing person, however, is not the same thing as having brought into being another example of that individual, given that a person is shaped as a person by other persons as they interact with him or her. Those others cannot be the same as the 'new' others who will now contribute to the personalizing of the new creature, regardless of its physical make up being biologically identical to the person from whom it is cloned. A process of differentiation is bound to unfold as soon as the new creature embarks on its existence as the interactions with its environment, especially the other people in that environment, take effect and shape the kind of person that they become.

There is plenty more to be said about the relational nature of personhood, relational with regard to other people, and 'the other' in general. Before we move in that direction, however, we should say a little more about why Christian belief places the whole matter in the context of our relation to God. We noted how the rise of modern science contributed to an embrace of the idea of personal freedom as something to be thought of individualistically. Part of the eagerness with which the idea of a 'Godless' freedom was embraced can be explained by the caricature of God that was being rejected. This was not only a view of God as the arch-spoilsport who punishes wrongdoers, the God who imposes his will on humankind in order to promote morally acceptable behaviour. It was also a conviction that any kind of God was, by definition, a sort of rival to humankind, whose being and activity crowded humankind out of the space which it should be able to count as its own.

Before attempting to lay bare the inadequacy of this idea of God (from the Christian perspective) we should note two points that can be made in mitigation of such ideas. The first is that the Christian church, in its chequered history of interference in politics and government, and in its flirtations with temporal power, has given any critical observer plenty of encouragement to look upon the Christian God as a tyrant interested more in banishing freedom than in gifting it. This is one of the baleful products of what historians of Christianity call the Constantinian mistake, the transformation of Christianity under the emperor Constantine from the 4th century AD onwards from a counter-cultural, underground liberation movement, rooted in the under-class of society, to a state endorsed, politically active, powerbroker to which anyone of ambition or wealth needed to belong.

The second mitigating factor is that if it is accepted that there is a God, some way must be found to conceive of God's being and activity in ways that protect the freedom of that which is not God. Critics of Christianity have argued that if God is omnipotent, omniscient, omni-present, and all the other 'omnis' that apparently define him as God, this means that there can be little room for human freedom if those qualities of God are actual and active. God is, so to speak, too big for there to be any room for anything else. The 'anything else' which is creation would simply have to do as it was told in the face of such an all-encompassing God. The alternative, from the atheistic point of view, is to assume that because there is in fact little scientific evidence of God's verifiable reality in accordance with his omnipotence (and all the other 'omnis'), we have no choice but to reject the notion of God and proceed to a future in which humankind assumes sole responsibility for itself and its environment. The field then becomes free for humankind to claim its freedom, or as we have seen, its apparent 'void'.

This portrait of God as all-knowing, all-powerful, all-encompassing, but somehow also remote, is unrecognisable from a Christian perspective, but that does not allow Christians to evade some responsibility for such ideas of God being so widespread, especially in contexts where Christianity has been dominant historically. The Christian church has itself sometimes operated with that kind of view, especially when it has wandered away from gospel-defined discipleship towards the gaining and exercise of temporal power. Neither is the shameful record limited only to the Constantinian era and the Middle Ages. There are plenty of manifestations of modern-day Christianity that have more to do with the attractions of power, wealth, status, and success than with self-sacrificial discipleship in the way of the cross.

Notwithstanding these mitigations, it is in fact the case that the conception of God as a rival to humankind, or as an impersonal enforcer of his will upon a reluctant victim, is radically contradicted by the Christian testimony concerning God. Not only does that testimony have very particular things to say about God, it also has important things to say about freedom, and how it should be understood in the light of who God is.

When we considered the significant implications of the idea that God created all that is out of nothing (*ex nihilo*) we noted that creation has its own being, as it is, as something other than God. It is not an emanation from him, nor is it controlled or regulated by the Creator such that it must unfold in a comprehensively pre-programmed way, having no freedom of its own. But we also noted that the Creator does not abandon creation to its own fate as if it were an astronaut cast adrift from his space capsule. Creation's own independence of being is not like that of a disgraced and disowned son, whose relationship with his origins is severed, even if understandably so. Notwithstanding the disordered condition that creation endures, which under another God might have resulted in its abandonment into disgrace, God rejects dis-grace as the determining condition of creation before its creator, in favour of grace, which is his own loving, saving action towards creation (*Ephesians 1: 9 – 10*). We find ourselves, again, visualising Irenaeus's analogy – that God relates graciously to his creation through his two hands, the Son and the Spirit.

The key word in this last sentence is 'graciously', an extension of the contrast we drew between disgrace and grace when attempting to distill the nature of God's relation to creation into a single idea. God engages with his creation unreservedly and comprehensively in that he himself (through the Son and the Spirit) is the bond that secures creation's sustaining and perfecting, but in such a way that creation's freedom is not violated. Indeed, the violation that forms the centrepiece of that engaging is that which is visited on the Son. The mighty actions of God in his re-creating, through the birth, life, death and resurrection of the Son, which in their cosmic significance can be matched only by creation itself, take shape in extreme humility. Humankind is gifted its eternal living destiny as something which, if it chooses, it can completely ignore or reject. Its freedom retains a kind of veto over God's tidal wave of love. George Herbert made this tension between humankind's freedom and God's self-sacrificial love the theme of his poem 'The Sacrifice' which sets out, in narrative poetic form, the Passion of Christ. These extracts give us a flavour of the whole:

Shame tears my soul, my bodie many a wound;
Sharp nails pierce this, but sharper that confound;
Reproaches, which are free, while I am bound.
                      Was ever grief like mine?

In healing not myself, there doth consist
All that salvation, which ye now resist;
Your safetie in my sicknesse doth subsist:
                      Was ever grief like mine?

(George Herbert, 'Sacrifice')

In our attending to some of the main ideas about personhood and freedom that are features of contemporary Western culture we have noted how they have been affected in their formation by, among other things, changing ideas about the place of God in our understandings of ourselves and our world. In connection with this we have also noted that, time and again, the notions of God that underlay the rejection of the transcendent or divine in favour of the divinising of humankind, in which humankind takes full responsibility for itself (at the expense of God) have been radically different from Christian understandings of God's being and nature. The God who has been scorned and rejected is not a God who is recognisable from a Christian viewpoint. To describe and account for all the ways in which ideas about the rejected God differ from a thoroughgoing Christian understanding of God would require a whole library of books. But the heart of the matter can be set out in a description of one major contradiction, which is that the rejected God has often been conceived deistically and monistically (a kind of singular, impersonal entity occupying the eternal, non-material realm) whereas the Christian understanding of God is that God is one God, who is three persons, Father, Son and Holy Spirit, in a relationship of perfect unity, and that the unity of the one God consists in the 'being in relation' of the eternal particularities of the persons of the Godhead. The fundamental importance of relationality in the Godhead can be seen when we realise that each of the persons has their particular being (as Father, as Son, and as Holy Spirit) in relation to the other persons. To speak of God as Father is not a way of bringing out a certain quality in God (his agency of creating, for example). It is, rather, to speak of the Person who is Father, in relationship with the Son and Spirit. To speak of God as Son is not a way of talking about God's project of saving or redeeming. It is to talk about the Person who is Son, in relationship with the Father and Spirit. To talk about God as Spirit is not to talk about the non-materiality of God, nor even the ability of God to impart life into creatures. It is to talk about the Person who is Holy Spirit, in relationship with the Father and the Son. God, in Christian understanding, is not an idea, or a concept, or an entity, or an extrapolation into immensity of what we might consider 'good'. God is not a 'What?' but a 'Who?' and this is because he is the living, personal God, whose own being is expressed through the eternal outpouring of love within the unity of divine personal fellowship which we see in the fountainhead of the loving Father, the obedience of the Son towards the Father in the power of the Spirit, and the overflowing, regenerating and perfecting work of the Spirit in creation which flows from the inner, loving, life of God, who is tri-personal, self-revealing, and savingly present, through the Son and the Spirit, to all that is other than Him.

In this brief, but somewhat dense, description of God's own being it can be seen that for such an account to do justice to its subject it has to employ the word 'person' or its adjectival derivative ('personal') whenever it focuses on God's essence – who God in fact is. Indeed, the connections between the idea of 'person' *per se* and Christian understandings of God's own nature go very deep. The very origins of the word 'person' are found in the fashioning by the early Christian theologians of a way of talking about God's engagement in dialogue, firstly within his own being, and then in relationship with those in creation whom he addresses as the God who speaks. As Joseph Ratzinger (Pope Benedict XVI) put it:

'The idea of person expresses in its origin the idea of dialogue and the idea of God as the dialogical being.' *(Joseph Ratzinger, 'Concerning the notion of person in theology,' Communio, Vo 17.3.)* When we think, in an everyday sense, of three persons being together, we tend to conceptualise this combination as three people or entities standing next to each other. To say that they then relate to one another is to envisage them as separate beings attending to other separate beings through sight, hearing, speaking, touching etc. The early Christian theologians decisively ruled out this kind of conception. They declared, as a result of their readings of Scripture, and their deep and prayerful reflections thereon, that the persons in God are relational in an absolute sense. By this they meant that being related to one another was not an added layer of existence, an 'extra' applied quality laid upon a deeper more original essence, like a golden chain worn by the three as a linking thread that having been put on could at any time be taken off. They meant that being in relation *is* the person itself. In its very nature the person exists only *as* relation. It was through this reflection on the meaning of 'person' that the church found itself able to gain a much deeper and more truthful understanding of what it means to say that God is Trinity – three Persons in one God. It also allows us to see that the Christian conception of 'person' is sharply different from the general secular or neutral use of the word and idea. For the Christian 'person' means 'relation', not just within descriptions of God's own being, but also in the everyday sense of the persons we are, meet, affect, and are affected by. In the secular context 'person' means 'the individual in his or her capacity as a possessor of reason and self-consciousness'. The fact that the use of the term 'person' has drifted away form its theological origins into a more generalised usage is a feature of cultural development. By looking back at the origins of the word we can gain a very helpful insight into the connection between Christian thought and a right understanding of who we are as persons because of the tri-personal reality of God himself. Peering into the mystery of God's own being as three Persons is not an activity that can in any sense be completed or finished. We should bear in mind the words of St Paul to the Corinthian church: 'For now, we see in a mirror, dimly, but then we will see face to face. Now, I know only in part; then I will know fully, even as I have been fully known.' *(I Cor 13: 12)* Trying to envisage just what it means to say that the one God is three Persons is a bit like trying to envisage what an undiscovered Mozart opera should sound like while holding in your hand an envelope on the back of which he scribbled just the names of the three main characters. However, listening to Mozart's music for a lifetime would improve your ability to make an informed guess as to what the new opera might sound like, and it would open up all sorts of pleasures along the way. It would also provide plenty of pointers towards what the new opera would *not* sound like. For the Christian a life of worship and service puts them in a place where the music of heaven becomes the soundtrack of life. They become 'otherworldly' not by dint of disengagement or ethereal relocation, but by being transformed, where they are, by the indwelling harmonies of God's own life made present by the Spirit of Christ. That is the spirit in which we have tried to look deeply into what God's being three Persons must mean for a better understanding of our own personhood. In fact we do not carry out our investigative theologising as an exercise in mere speculation. We are not shooting in the dark, because we are drawn by Scripture itself, and the Spirit's prompting, to attend to what God is saying about himself. To proceed in Christian living and believing as if we were left entirely to our own devices would be to position ourselves above God, as if a true knowledge of

God were simply a matter of deploying our own intelligence to greater effectiveness. To return to the Mozart analogy, it is, rather, as if Mozart himself is alongside, prompting insights and intimations on a pathway of discovery.

Recognising that the concept of 'person' has its roots in the Christian revelation that God is a trinity of persons in dialogue, and that the meaning of 'person' is 'relation', allows us to approach an apprehension of God's own being that is both truthful and dumbfounding. We find ourselves in a state of awe that is not so very different from the witness that the mystic tradition of contemplation gives us as exemplified by St John of the Cross (see Chapter 3 above). To contemplate the glory of God as he is in himself, an eternal choreography of the giving and receiving of love between the divine persons, is a necessary function, or even product, of Christian worship.

God's own life in relation therefore forms the basis of our understanding of why human beings are persons and not just human beings. However, notwithstanding the hugely important insight into God's own being that 'person' as 'relation' brings, we would do well to be aware of the danger of stopping at this point, in awestruck wonder at the scene we have been contemplating – as if the dance of God's life of love is like a party going on in the house next door, to which we are not invited, and we are peering in from the outside at a self-sustaining and self-referential event that is a phantasmagoria of colour, music and celebration, totally oblivious of, and unconcerned about, anything that is outside of its own experience.

In his contemplation of the inner dynamic of God's life as a trinity of persons in relationship St Augustine called the Spirit the bond of love between the Father and the Son (as we have already noted in Chapter 2). We can see how he might have arrived at this conception in that it is much easier to conceive of the Father and the Son as being persons (in the natural or secular sense) but more difficult to see the Spirit in those terms. Much easier therefore to envisage the Spirit as some kind of immaterial energy or force, or, in fact, 'bond'. It also makes it much more likely that we would conceive of the life of the trinity as being self-enclosed, a kind of pairing, in which the Father and the Son face each other while the Spirit acts as 'enabler'. This is not a million miles away from the difference between a romantic meeting of two people, absorbed in their being together, and the entirely different dynamic that applies when three people come together. This is not to imply that the loving life of God's own being is in any way romantic. It is just to make a comparison with our human experience, and to highlight the limitations of Augustine's description of the Trinity. In contrast to this tendency towards introspection that Augustine's proposal suggests other elaborations of the inner life of God have highlighted God's orientation to the outward, as opposed to the inward. This is based on taking seriously the particularity of each of the persons of the Godhead in which what they each distinctively, but not exclusively, do (create, redeem and perfect) is seen to be intrinsic to their very being as the persons who are Father, Son and Spirit. We can see how these actions of creating (Father), redeeming (Son) and perfecting (Spirit) are all actions directed outwards towards what is other than God, and because there can never be any contradiction between what God does and what God is we can say that God is, in his own being, the Self-Giver. The Persons are emphatically not 'self-oriented' but 'self-giving'. In other words, God is the one who in his very nature is overflowingly centrifugal and not tightly centripetal. There are no boundaries enclosing that party next door. The dazzling light, the achingly beautiful music and the loving speech radiate outwards, drawing all who hear and see to come and be part of what is going on. If the Spirit has a distinctive role in the loving life of God it is to configure the love of Father for Son, and Son for Father, as not merely a mark of God's own perfect life, but a life-giving presence in creation drawing creation itself to its own perfecting as it comes to know, by the work of the Spirit, the power of love *(John 15: 26, 16: 13 – 15)*.

Most descriptions of the biblical account of personhood place the concept of our being made 'in the image of God' *(Gen 1: 27)* at the heart of their accounts. That is right and proper. At the same time, it is reasonable to suggest that in their eagerness to engage with that powerful and well-known phrase many of those accounts have taken their lead from what they consider to be the characteristic qualities that humans possess which set them apart from the rest of the animal kingdom – especially the ability to reason. They then identify this characteristic as being in some sense a 'spark of the divine' in humankind, leading to an over-optimistic attitude towards humankind's ability to manage itself and whatever else it seeks to control through its intellectual capacities. Because we can think and reason, this apparently becomes the pointer towards our being made in God's image. It has the knock-on effect, of course, of turning God into a sort of giant Mind, perhaps the super-computer to end all super-computers.

But if God is not a giant Mind, but, rather, a united fellowship of Father, Son and Spirit, three persons in one God, whose own being consists in relation, our being made in the image of this God has little to do with reason or thinking, but everything to do with personhood and relation. We, as persons, do not make ourselves in isolation or individuality. We are made by the myriad connections in relation that make up our lives as they are lived with, and for, and at the hands of, others. As we have already acknowledged in our reference to what a biography denuded of all references to interactions with significant others would look like (chapter 3), we form and are formed by the huge cast list that would scroll up the screen at the end of the film of our life, all those people without whom it would not be possible to portray the drama of which we were the central character. And if our analogy of the inner life of this triune God as a dazzling, haunting, overflowing party which can be heard and seen throughout creation has any truth in it, we should accept that this carries immense implications for the body of persons, the Church, which is graciously enabled to partake of the life of that party, so that it can be a sign to the rest of creation. To what extent is the church's own life a reflection of the inner life of this God who is the overflowing perfection of relation? Does the theme tune of heaven echo harmoniously throughout creation through the life of the church as it lives in and for creation's perfecting *(Romans 8:19 – 21)*? Or is the music of the life of the church too often a cacophony of competitive self-trumpeting?

Attempting to form a picture of God's own triune being that is at least to some extent faithful to the Scriptures and the Christian tradition, and in so doing start to grasp a little of what it means to say that we are 'persons', we have talked about the three Persons in God in fairly general terms. If we are to become more specific in our quest for guidance regarding the full dimensions of meaning in the word 'person' from the Christian perspective the next step, not surprisingly, is to look in the direction of the Person who is Son.

The heart of the Christian gospel is to be found, of course, in the Person who is Son, who is Jesus Christ. From the earliest years of its existence, in the aftermath of the crucifixion and resurrection, the church has been engaged in a process of coming to terms with exactly who Jesus is and how, in him, God is present within his creation. On the way to affirming that Jesus is fully man and fully God (as declared in the Christian creeds hammered out in the fourth and fifth centuries) alternative understandings of him were elaborated but, eventually, rejected. These were that Jesus was, on the one hand, simply a very good man, indeed the best that there had ever been, imbued with wisdom, courage and a unique 'God-consciousness', but not divine. Over on the opposite extreme was the rival opinion that although Jesus of Nazareth had the outward appearance of a human being, his actual being was divine. His life in this world was therefore a kind of pretence, an interlude, an excursion, during which the contingencies of earthly existence could not really impact on him because he was insulated from such indignities by his divine status.

There is evidence that the instinct to favour the divine over the human emerged quite early in the Christian era through the writing of what came to be known as apocryphal gospels; accounts of Jesus' life and ministry that exaggerated his divine status and powers. It is very instructive to note how the early church dealt with the instinct to heighten the sense of Jesus' specialness as a method of reinforcing the truth of his divinity as displayed in these texts written, mostly, in the second century AD. One area of contention was that of Jesus' own biographical background. It was almost inevitable that people would start to circulate stories about Jesus' early life that 'proved' or supported his divine origins and status.

These accounts rely heavily on stories about Jesus' childhood in which the miraculous dimension is very prominent so that he is shown, apparently, to be divine. One of the stories describes Jesus as a young boy playing with his friends in the mud at the edge of a stream. They use the mud to fashion toy birds, leaving them to dry in the sun. Everyone else's toy birds remain exactly that – miniature avian statues standing stock still by the water's edge. But (surprise, surprise!) the mud birds made by Jesus spread their wings and lift off into the sky above, singing and swooping in honour of their divine creator.

You can see the logic. If this really was the Son of God amongst us he must have been a divine being from the beginning and therefore above the material limitations that the rest of humanity struggles with. He looked human, but really he was God in disguise. So they felt bound to fill in the gaps in his early life by constructing stories that 'proved' his divinity.

But the early church rejected this approach. That is why such stories do not feature in the New Testament. In the actual Gospels Jesus' personality is certainly not underplayed. He does indeed have a remarkable impact on the people he meets. Even tough, down to earth fishermen are intrigued by his charismatic presence and his visionary message. But nowhere is the impression created in the New Testament gospels that this was some sort of alien, some kind of avatar figure, who didn't really belong in the dust and dirt of this world. In fact, when Jesus started his preaching ministry in and near his hometown, his hearers' response was to say 'Is this not Joseph's son?' *(Luke 4:22)* – a reaction both to his humble origins, of which they were very aware, and his pointed criticism of their empty religion. They were not awestruck by the presence in their midst of a god. They were scandalised by the truth-telling of the young man that used to live round the corner – whose father was everyone's favourite furniture maker.

Nuanced versions of these extreme positions, Jesus the merely very good man, and the divine Jesus who only looked and sounded like a man, were part of the debating scene in the early Christian era and modern versions still make their claims even today, such is the perennial fascination with the carpenter's son from Nazareth.

The church fathers of the early Christian centuries realised that at the heart of the issue lay the effectiveness of the salvation that Jesus' life, death, and resurrection had apparently achieved. They saw that if God's becoming a man (the man Jesus of Nazareth) was to have a universal salvific effect, his becoming that man must be genuine and complete, so that the whole of the human condition is renewed and set on a path towards its perfecting. This would disqualify the 'divine being who is only wearing the appearance of a human' option, of course, because the becoming human would be inauthentic.

The same problem arises for the 'Jesus the mere man with an extraordinary God-consciousness' interpretations because they also leave our materiality unaffected as they concentrate on example, ethics, feelings and 'the spiritual'. That is the problem for all over-spiritualized interpretations of Jesus. Crucially, they have no need of the bodily resurrection of the crucified one, because the material realm is not where it's at, apparently. So, the resurrection is thought of as a spiritual event or experience, rather than a physical one, a kind of parable of the apparent superiority of the psychological and spiritual over the lowly material.

Something of the feel of the disturbing offence that physical decay and death has in its despoiling of God's good creation can be seen in Jesus' reaction to the death of his friend Lazarus (John 11: 1 – 44). There is the stench of death, quite literally ('Lord, there is already a stench, because he has been dead for four days.' v 39) and Jesus is visibly agitated at both the stark ugliness of the outworking of creation's imprisonment in disorder, of which death is the outcome and sign, and, presumably, a kind of shuddering in himself at the scale of the battle he must soon face in the vanquishing of death by his own death. The material realities of Jesus' life stand front and centre in the gospel accounts. Trying to construct a case for a 'spiritual' reading of the story of Jesus simply runs against the grain of that story, in which stones, water, bread, fish, sand, corpses, wood, nails, thorns and scars function as its reference points and its raw material.

The disqualification of the 'good man, whose highly tuned 'God-consciousness' stood as an example to others' also arises from this Jesus being fully human, but only human. He identifies with God, to an unprecedented degree, but he is not himself God. If that is the case it becomes impossible to see how anything has actually been achieved or changed because of him that will bring about the transformation of the whole of creation, an ambition and possibility that only the Creator himself could entertain and realise.

Among the early church fathers who worried away at the conundrum of the Incarnation of the Son of God was St Gregory of Nazianzus. He, along with other great minds in the church, established what was to become the definitive understanding of what was happening in and through Jesus, which was that as God, Jesus could, and did indeed bring into effect the transformative re-creating that creation needed, and that this could only be achieved if he was himself fully human, experiencing all that it means to be human, except the giving in to the temptation of sin *(Hebrews 4: 15)*. As a result, humankind, which is the crown and custodian of creation *(Genesis 1: 26 – 28, Psalm 8 etc),* can be re-made according to God's perfecting purpose, thereby allowing the rest of creation to be released into its own perfecting In Him *(Romans 8: 19 – 24)*.

Gregory of Nazianzus's summary of the importance of the humanity of the Son of God was expressed in his famous declaration which stated that 'that which is not assumed is not redeemed.' In other words, Jesus must be fully human, with no pretence, and in no way partial, in order that our full salvation can be secured, and not thwarted by some irredeemable residue or remainder which he either chose not to, or was unable to, embrace. At his incarnation, the Son took to himself the *fallen* human nature that we all share – not some approximation of it, or some idealised version of it, but the very stuff of which we are made and in which we see the stain of death.

The author of the Letter to the Hebrews, aware, no doubt, of the unlikeliness of the Christian proclamation regarding Jesus, both to Jewish traditionalists and agnostic onlookers, placed Jesus' status and calling at the centre of his argument. The astounding claim that in this man God was present to heal and transform is spelt out in the early parts of his discourse. He is 'the reflection of God's glory and the exact imprint of God's very being, and he sustains all things by his powerful word.' *(Hebrews 1:3)*. Here is the fully divine Son of God, who because of his divinity is qualified to renew all creation, the enterprise whose beginnings he, as Son of God, was instrumentally involved in *(John 1:1 etc)*. Yet just a few sentences further on the author of the letter, speaking of the same person who has just been described as bearing the imprint of God's very being, now describes Jesus of Nazareth as having to be like his brothers and sisters in all respects i.e. a real man, in order for his life, death and resurrection to achieve the atonement of his people through the forgiveness of their sins *(Hebrews 2: 17)*. A little further on he elaborates the significance of Jesus' real humanity by linking him with our own experience as weak humans:

'For we do not have a high priest who is unable to sympathize with our weaknesses, but we have one who in every respect has been tested as we are, yet without sin.' *(Hebrews 4:15)*

It is probably fair to say that many Christians approach the acceptance of Jesus' full humanity with a degree of uncertainty. This can be because their life 'before Jesus' (dark) and 'after Jesus' (light) has been strikingly and even dramatically different. Only God himself in the person of his divine Son could have brought about such a miraculous change, and this is, of course, utterly authentic and valid. Other Christians, whose path to faith has not been so dramatic, or whose style of worship is less extrovert, may also feel the same uncertainty about Jesus' humanity, simply because they have always taken Jesus to be God among us, doing what he did because of his divinity (healing the sick, raising the dead etc) and thereby demonstrating his difference from us who are thoroughly ordinary, by contrast. Thinking of Jesus as a man becomes almost the same as thinking of him as a mere man.

The key to all this is the Holy Spirit. As we have seen, the Son of God does not live his incarnate life as if he were the special and sole occupant of a kind of armoured personnel carrier issued from the armoury of heaven for the purposes of a special operation on the battlefield of earth. He enters the fray equipped with nothing more than what we all have – the helpless and vulnerable form of a newborn. He grows and comes to adult maturity, 'increasing in wisdom... and divine and human favour' *(Luke 2: 52)*. When the time is right he submits himself to John's baptism, at which the Spirit descends upon him, the same Spirit who then leads him into the wilderness to be tempted.

So begins the distinctive and essential career of a *man*, living in complete fulfillment of the will of God, through the enabling of the Spirit. This is the Second Adam, living his human life as it was intended that the first Adam should, in the Spirit enabled reality of obedience and humility rather than disobedience and spurious independence, thereby forging, once and for all, the template intended for human life on which the destiny of creation can now be founded.

It is, again, the author of the Letter to the Hebrews who shows us how this Son and Spirit 'partnership in achievement' then plays out on our behalf. Having set forth the contours of God's covenantal commitment to creation in and through his Son, which supersedes the preparatory purpose of his earlier covenant in the law, and the golden thread of faith in this God that runs through the story of Israel, the writer then connects it all to us:

Therefore, since we are surrounded by so great a cloud of witnesses, let us also lay aside every weight and the sin that clings so closely, and let us run with perseverance the race that is set before us, looking to Jesus the pioneer and perfecter of our faith, who for the sake of the joy that was set before him endured the cross, disregarding its shame, and has taken his seat at the right hand of the throne of God. *(Hebrews 12: 1 – 2)*

The key phrase is 'pioneer and perfecter of our faith'. In other words, Jesus' own life of faith, the human life he lived in the power of the Spirit, is what makes possible the life of faith that his followers are called to live. They follow him as the one who pioneered that Spirit-enabled pathway which leads to the Father, just as the lesser members of a mountaineering team follow the leader who strikes out ahead of them, thereby defining the route they must follow to the summit.

'Sitting at the feet of Jesus' is a well-worn metaphor for pietistic quietude, justifiable in some limited contexts (Martha and Mary, *Luke 10: 38 – 42*). Far more useful, and theologically robust, is the metaphor of walking in his pioneering footsteps because those footsteps are for us to follow. There may be times when sitting is required, but the wider reality is that a Christian is a person of the Way (the original identifier was 'people of The Way' – *Acts 9:2*). She presses forward to that which lies ahead, the homecoming in the presence of the Father where the pioneering Son, in the power of the Spirit, has gone before.

Therefore it is in the incarnate Son that the full outline of personhood is displayed in our earthly context, part of the history of the world. In him we see the outworking of 'person' as 'relation' as it takes its form in the life of Jesus of Nazareth in his honouring of the Father through the enabling of the Spirit. We see the sheer scale of the Spirit's enabling in that as his empowering plays out, its result is the ever-sharpening delineation of the man Jesus. The Spirit's enabling does not lead to his humanity being taken over or obscured. The Spirit's enabling matches exactly the self-effacing character of the Spirit as, by his presence and power, the Son's own particularity comes into ever sharper focus because of the activity of the Spirit.

It is this distinctively self-effacing activity of the Spirit that allows us to see that 'person as relation', the full meaning of 'person' as it is seen in the Godhead, does not result in a dilution of the particular persons who together constitute the Godhead. The Persons do not fall out of focus. We might expect such a dilution because of the apparent prioritizing of 'relation', with its connotations of plurality and its focus on the 'whole' as opposed to the 'parts'. Talking of God as 'Trinity' seems, to our humanly limited perception, to be tantamount to focusing on the apparent plurality in God at the expense of the individual members of the divine fellowship of being. In reality, relation becomes the context in which grace illuminates and delineates the Son in his filial obedience, the Father in his loving fatherhood and the Spirit in his enabling and perfecting. Particularity is the essence of relation through the gracious honouring of the other which is the life of God.

By taking a little time to concentrate on this dynamic, in which relation is intimately tied up with particularity, we can see how we are beginning to come full circle, and in sight of the place where we started, in our consideration of what personhood actually is. That starting point was 'freedom', and we counted it as being at the heart of any conception of what the term 'person' in fact means. We saw, at the end of the previous chapter, through the Japanese girl's wonderful metaphor of the walled garden, how submission to God in Christ by the indwelling of the Spirit, far from entailing the loss of freedom, in fact proves to be liberation *into* freedom, the only freedom that is worth having, because it is the gracious gift of the one who made us to experience the freedom of his fellowship which unbinds us from the prison of self-absorption.

This remarkable but undeniable reality is summed up by St Paul in his own distillation of what the gospel means for the disciple of Christ – 'Now the Lord is the Spirit, and where the Spirit of the Lord is, there is freedom' *(2 Corinthians 3: 17).* It is a commonplace in Christian testimony that as a result of the experience of the grace of God in Christ through the Spirit the Christian person is revealed as being not less than the old familiar self, but more than that self; more authentically the person that they have potentially been, and are now becoming. (We noted this phenomenon when thinking about God's involvement in the formation of the Holy Scriptures as the natural is taken up into the supernatural, and thereby perfected).

What was formerly a suggestion, an approximation, a faded black and white photo, is now a technicolour, fully focused, 3D realization of who that person is. Friends are likely to say 'So *that's* what God meant by 'George/Jane/Ashok/Maria….'

Therefore we are talking not about freedom as an idea, or an elusive quality that must be acquired or grasped, or some kind of state into which the person must step having managed to extricate themselves from the chains of their former existence. We are talking about a *shaped* freedom, freedom which has a particular form and substance, the very opposite of the void that we identified as the outcome of modern/post-modern, secular conceptions of freedom. That shape is defined by the tri-personal God whose gift this freedom is.

A major implication of person being relation, as set out in God, and as echoed in our ideal experience, is that, as we have seen, particularity is affirmed in relationship. This is good for our understanding of ourselves as particular persons (whose particular personhood is on the way to perfecting in Christ, by the indwelling Spirit). But it is also good for our understanding of community. Community that is brought into being by the grace of God (which is a definition of the term 'church') is not like a battalion all dressed in the same uniform lined up in straight rows. It is not a uniform community, made to look and behave all alike. It is a diverse community, brought into being by the grace of God, which means that it is the result of free human choice made possible by the Spirit. Not so much a military battalion as an association or free assembly of infinitely varied members, different in age, appearance, culture and capacities.

There is much talk in Western cultural contexts of the importance of 'community', or, rather, there is much use of the term 'community' *per se*, but not as a way of describing the whole of society. Society itself tends, in contemporary Western thought, to be sub-divided into self-contained 'communities', defined by generalized immutable concepts such as skin colour, or sexual/gender identity, as if such over-simplified identification is all that is required for talk about persons in relation.

The Christian conception of 'community' stands in direct contradiction of that model. Whenever St Paul talks about the Spirit at work in the life of the church he focuses as much on diversity as on unity – an expression of the mutually supportive connection between particularity and relation that is enabled by grace. So, 'there are varieties of gifts, but the same Spirit, and there are varieties of service, but the same Lord, and there are varieties of working but it is the same God who inspires them all in everyone.' *(1 Corinthians 12: 4 – 6)*. This is why, in Christian conception, 'there is no longer Jew or Greek, there is no longer slave or free, there is no longer male or female; for all of you are one in Jesus Christ.' *(Galatians 3:28)*

It is to the church's shame that so much of its own history is a contradiction of this truth, both by the imposition of uniformity as a false short-cut to unity, and through its unwillingness to express true diversity in the midst of societal norms which segregate humanity into separated 'communities'. Perhaps this helps to explain why the church has lost its cutting edge in contexts where societal polarization is more apparent than integrity and openness to the other.

At a time when, in so many settings, it is truer than ever that a person can 'make something of themselves' it is perhaps even more important that we should understand the connection between our particularity and our freedom in relation. As the particular persons that we are we have the freedom to pursue personal achievement and realization. The secular world especially holds out this opportunity as a defining characteristic of what human life is or should be.

St Paul, however, gives us a glimpse into what a Christian can say about themselves in the light of the grace of God who takes responsibility for our making, as we rejoice in God's gift of freedom through which we play our own part in that making. Having lamented his record as a former persecutor of the church he frames his self-understanding in the context of God's activity in and through the man that he is:

'But by the grace of God I am what I am, and his grace towards me has not been in vain. On the contrary, I worked harder than any of them, - though it was not I, but the grace of God that is with me.' *(1 Corinthians 15:10)*

Let us then attend to what one of the wisest commentators on the human condition has said about the possibilities of life that stretch before anyone who is interested in 'making something of themselves'. Here is Dietrich Bonhoeffer in his *Letters and Papers from Prison*, having just had a conversation with a French priest about their respective ambitions – the priest to 'become a saint', Bonhoeffer to 'learn to have faith':

'I didn't realise the depth of the contrast……I discovered later, and I'm still discovering right up to this moment. That it is only by living completely in this world that one learns to have faith. One must completely abandon any attempt to make something of oneself, whether it be a saint or a converted sinner, or a church-man (a so-called priestly type!), a righteous man, or an unrighteous one, a sick man or a healthy one. By this-worldliness I mean living unreservedly in life's duties, problems, successes and failures, experiences and perplexities. In so doing we throw ourselves completely into the arms of God, taking seriously not our own sufferings, but those of God in the world – watching with Christ in Gethsemane. That, I think. Is faith…..' *(quoted by David Ford and Daniel Hardy, 'Living in Praise,' 2005, p110).*

Printed in Poland
by Amazon Fulfillment
Poland Sp. z o.o., Wrocław
02 May 2023

a2fae010-3579-4ca3-a9fb-b2de41404d47R01